THE SPIRIT OF CHRISTMAS
COOKBOOK
Volume 3

From appetizers and nibbles to sweet surprises, the Spirit of Christmas Cookbook *helps you create visions of sugarplums and wondrous feasts for your Yuletide table. Among the many luscious selections are chocolate-drenched candies with scrumptious cherry centers, a succulent stuffed turkey breast smothered in cranberry-port sauce, and a delicately nutty torte topped with a holly frosting wreath. Spicy Creole-style oysters in pastry shells are perfect open house fare, and our sweet bread wreath is a memorable gift. More than 240 recipes such as these make this third treasury of our favorite foods a valuable source of inspiration for your holiday cooking. As you search for ways to share your joy during this festive season, turn to our kitchen-tested recipes to carry the spirit of Christmas to those you love and cherish.*

LEISURE ARTS, INC.
Little Rock, Arkansas

THE SPIRIT OF CHRISTMAS

COOKBOOK

Volume 3

EDITORIAL STAFF

Vice President and Editor-in-Chief: Anne Van Wagner Childs
Executive Director: Sandra Graham Case
Test Kitchen Director/Foods Editor: Celia Fahr Harkey, R.D.
Editorial Director: Susan Frantz Wiles
Creative Art Director: Gloria Bearden
Senior Graphics Art Director: Melinda Stout

FOODS
Assistant Foods Editor: Jane Kenner Prather
Test Kitchen Home Economist: Rose Glass Klein
Test Kitchen Coordinator: Nora Faye Taylor
Test Kitchen Assistants: Camille T. Alstadt and
  Melissa Adams

EDITORIAL
Managing Editor: Linda L. Trimble
Associate Editor: Janice Teipen Wojcik
Assistant Editors: Terri Leming Davidson and
  Stacey Robertson Marshall

ART
Book/Magazine Graphics Art Director: Diane M. Hugo
Production Artists: Linda Chambers, Wendy Lair, and
  Michael A. Spigner
Photography Stylist: Karen Smart Hall

PROMOTIONS
Managing Editors: Alan Caudle and Marjorie Ann Lacy
Associate Editors: Debby Carr, Ellen J. Clifton, Steve M.
  Cooper, Dixie L. Morris, and Beth Stark
Designer: Dale Rowett
Art Director: Linda Lovette Smart
Publishing Systems Administrator: Cindy Lumpkin
Publishing Systems Assistants: Susan Mary Gray and
  Robert Walker

BUSINESS STAFF

Publisher: Rick Barton
Vice President and General Manager: Thomas L. Carlisle
Vice President, Finance: Tom Siebenmorgen
Vice President, Retail Marketing: Bob Humphrey
Vice President, National Accounts: Pam Stebbins
Retail Marketing Director: Margaret Sweetin

General Merchandise Manager: Cathy Laird
Vice President, Operations: Brian U. Davis
Distribution Director: Rob Thieme
Retail Customer Service Director: Tonie B. Maulding
Retail Customer Service Managers: Carolyn Pruss and
  Wanda Price
Print Production Manager: Fred F. Pruss

We would like to extend our thanks to Christy Kalder, Micah McConnell, Susan Warren Reeves, R.D., and Kay Wright for their contributions as former foods editors and consultants for *The Spirit of Christmas* and *Memories in the Making* volumes from which we chose our recipes.

Library of Congress Catalog Card Number 97-73650
International Standard Book Number 1-57486-124-7

TABLE OF CONTENTS

TABLE OF CONTENTS
(Continued)

TABLE OF CONTENTS
(Continued)

GIFTS OF GOOD TASTE 138

SANTA'S SWEETSHOP

Sharing sugary morsels is a time-honored way to spread Yuletide joy. Inspired by Santa's North Pole sweetshop, we've assembled a tempting array of delicacies — candies, cookies, fudges, and more — that say "season's greetings" to friends and family. You'll be amazed at the variety that can be made in your own kitchen. From ooey-gooey chewies to coffee-dunking crisps, these mouth-watering treats will please everyone in your holiday household who has a sweet tooth, including the jolly old elf himself!

Lacy patterns of royal icing create the look of delicate crochet atop tangy Lemon Snowflake Cookies (recipe on page 9). A fluted-edge cookie cutter gives the citrusy cookies their scalloped border, and a pastry bag is used for the dotted icing.

Pecan-Cinnamon Cookies (clockwise from top left) are bursting with nuts. A delicious variation on a Southern *favorite, Chewy Pecan Squares taste like miniature pecan pies! Coffee-flavored Mocha Crunch Cookies have loads of chocolate mini chips.*

LEMON SNOWFLAKE COOKIES

(Shown on pages 6 and 7)

COOKIES

- 1/2 cup butter or margarine, softened
- 1 cup sugar
- 1 egg
- 2 tablespoons milk
- 1 teaspoon grated lemon zest
- 1/2 teaspoon lemon extract
- 2 cups all-purpose flour
- 1/2 teaspoon baking soda
- 1/2 teaspoon cream of tartar
- 1/4 teaspoon salt

ROYAL ICING

- 1 3/4 cups sifted confectioners sugar
- 2 tablespoons warm water
- 1 tablespoon meringue powder
- 1/8 teaspoon lemon extract

For cookies, cream butter and sugar in a large bowl until fluffy. Add egg, milk, lemon zest, and lemon extract; beat until smooth. In a small bowl, combine remaining ingredients; add to creamed mixture and stir until a soft dough forms. Wrap in plastic wrap and chill 2 hours or until dough is firm.

Preheat oven to 375 degrees. On a lightly floured surface, use a floured rolling pin to roll out dough to 1/8-inch thickness. Use a 3-inch-diameter fluted-edge cookie cutter to cut out cookies. Transfer to a lightly greased baking sheet. Bake 8 to 10 minutes or until bottoms of cookies are lightly browned. Transfer to a wire rack to cool completely.

For royal icing, beat confectioners sugar, water, meringue powder, and lemon extract in a medium bowl with an electric mixer 7 to 10 minutes or until stiff. Spoon icing into a pastry bag fitted with a small round tip. Pipe snowflake design on each cookie. Allow icing to harden. Store in an airtight container.

Yield: about 2 1/2 dozen cookies

PECAN-CINNAMON COOKIES

- 1/2 cup vegetable shortening
- 1/4 cup butter or margarine, softened
- 1 cup firmly packed brown sugar
- 1/4 cup light corn syrup
- 1 egg
- 1 tablespoon vanilla extract
- 2 cups all-purpose flour
- 2 teaspoons ground cinnamon
- 1 teaspoon baking soda
- 1/2 teaspoon salt
- 1 1/2 cups chopped pecans, toasted

Preheat oven to 350 degrees. In a medium bowl, cream shortening, butter, and brown sugar until fluffy. Add corn syrup, egg, and vanilla; beat until smooth. In a small bowl, combine flour, cinnamon, baking soda, and salt. Add dry ingredients to creamed mixture; stir until a soft dough forms. Stir in pecans. Drop tablespoonfuls of dough 2 inches apart onto a greased baking sheet. Bake 8 to 10 minutes or until bottoms are lightly browned. Allow cookies to cool on pan 5 minutes; transfer to a wire rack to cool completely. Store in an airtight container.

Yield: about 4 dozen cookies

MOCHA CRUNCH COOKIES

- 1/2 cup butter or margarine, softened
- 1/4 cup vegetable shortening
- 1/2 cup plus 2 tablespoons granulated sugar, divided
- 1/2 cup firmly packed brown sugar
- 1 egg yolk
- 1 1/2 teaspoons vanilla extract
- 1 3/4 cups all-purpose flour
- 1 tablespoon instant coffee granules
- 1/4 teaspoon baking powder
- 1/4 teaspoon baking soda
- 1/4 teaspoon salt
- 1/2 cup semisweet chocolate mini chips

Preheat oven to 375 degrees. In a large bowl, cream butter, shortening,

1/2 cup granulated sugar, and brown sugar until fluffy. Add egg yolk and vanilla; beat until smooth. In a small bowl, combine flour, instant coffee, baking powder, baking soda, and salt. Add dry ingredients to creamed mixture; stir until a soft dough forms. Stir in chocolate chips. Shape dough into 1-inch balls; place 2 inches apart on an ungreased baking sheet. Flatten cookies with bottom of a glass dipped in remaining 2 tablespoons granulated sugar. Bake 10 to 12 minutes or until edges are lightly browned. Allow cookies to cool on pan 2 minutes; transfer cookies to a wire rack to cool completely. Store in an airtight container.

Yield: about 4 dozen cookies

CHEWY PECAN SQUARES

CRUST

- 1 package (18 1/4 ounces) yellow cake mix
- 1 egg
- 1/3 cup vegetable oil

FILLING

- 1 cup sugar
- 4 eggs
- 1/2 teaspoon salt
- 1 cup dark corn syrup
- 1/4 cup butter or margarine, melted
- 1 teaspoon vanilla extract
- 2 cups chopped pecans

Preheat oven to 350 degrees. For crust, combine cake mix, egg, and oil in a medium bowl. Press mixture into bottom of a greased 9 x 13-inch baking pan. Bake 20 minutes.

For filling, beat sugar, eggs, and salt in a large bowl until well blended. Beat in corn syrup, melted butter, and vanilla. Stir in pecans. Pour over hot crust. Bake at 350 degrees 30 to 35 minutes or until brown around edges and center is set. Cool completely. Cut into 1 1/2-inch squares. Store in an airtight container.

Yield: about 3 dozen squares

Traditional German Springerle (clockwise from top) are ideal for dunking in coffee or cocoa. The raised designs on this licorice-flavored cookie are made with a springerle rolling pin or cookie molds. Yummy White Chocolate Cookies have whimsical Christmas tree designs made with piped-on chocolate batter. Chocolate-Orange Logs are melt-in-your-mouth wonderful.

CHOCOLATE-ORANGE LOGS

COOKIES
1	cup butter or margarine, softened
1	cup sugar
1	egg
1	teaspoon grated orange zest
2 1/4	cups all-purpose flour
1	teaspoon baking powder

ICING
1/2	cup semisweet chocolate chips
1	teaspoon vegetable shortening
1/4	teaspoon orange extract
3/4	cup finely chopped pecans

For cookies, cream butter and sugar in a large bowl until fluffy. Add egg and orange zest; beat until smooth. In a medium bowl, combine flour and baking powder. Add dry ingredients to creamed mixture; stir until a soft dough forms.

Spoon mixture into a pastry bag fitted with a large star tip (we used tip #6B). Pipe 2 1/2-inch strips of dough 2 inches apart onto an ungreased baking sheet. Chill cookies 30 minutes.

Preheat oven to 375 degrees. Bake about 8 minutes or until golden and firm. Allow cookies to cool on pan 2 minutes; transfer to a wire rack to cool completely.

For icing, place chocolate chips and shortening in a small microwave-safe bowl; microwave on medium power (50%) 3 minutes or until chips are soft. Stir chips until smooth; stir in orange extract. Dip one end of each cookie in chocolate mixture and then in pecans. Place on waxed paper; allow chocolate to harden. Store in an airtight container.

Yield: about 5 dozen cookies

SPRINGERLE

Make cookies at least 2 weeks in advance to allow flavor to develop.

4	eggs
2	cups sugar
1	teaspoon grated lemon zest
1	teaspoon anise extract **or** 2 teaspoons anise seed, crushed
3 3/4	cups all-purpose flour
1	teaspoon baking powder

In a large bowl, beat eggs at high speed of an electric mixer 1 minute. Gradually add sugar, beating at high speed 10 minutes. Add lemon zest and anise extract. In a medium bowl, combine flour and baking powder. Stir dry ingredients into egg mixture (dough will be stiff). Shape dough into 2 balls. Wrap in plastic wrap and chill 1 hour.

Work with 1 ball of dough at a time. On a lightly floured surface, use a floured rolling pin to roll out dough into a 1/4-inch-thick rectangle the width of a springerle rolling pin. Pressing firmly, roll designs into dough using springerle rolling pin (or press dough into individual cookie molds). If using rolling pin, cut out cookies along design lines (a pizza cutter works well). Place cookies on a lightly greased baking sheet; allow to stand uncovered at room temperature overnight.

Preheat oven to 350 degrees. Place baking sheet in oven; immediately reduce temperature to 300 degrees. Bake 15 to 20 minutes or until bottoms are lightly browned. Transfer cookies to a wire rack to cool completely. Store in an airtight container.

Yield: about 7 1/2 dozen cookies

WHITE CHOCOLATE COOKIES

3/4	cup butter or margarine, softened and divided
1/4	cup vegetable shortening
1/2	cup granulated sugar
1/2	cup firmly packed brown sugar
1	egg yolk
1/2	teaspoon vanilla extract
1 1/3	cups plus 6 tablespoons all-purpose flour, divided
1/2	teaspoon baking powder
1/8	teaspoon salt
1/2	cup coarsely chopped walnuts
2	ounces white chocolate, coarsely chopped
1	tablespoon chocolate-flavored syrup

In a large bowl, beat 1/2 cup butter and shortening until well blended; add sugars and beat until fluffy. Add egg yolk and vanilla; beat until smooth. In a small bowl, combine 1 1/3 cups flour, baking powder, and salt. In a food processor, process walnuts and chocolate until finely ground. Add dry ingredients and walnut mixture to creamed mixture; stir until a soft dough forms. Wrap in plastic wrap and chill 1 to 2 hours.

Preheat oven to 350 degrees. Shape chilled dough into 3/4-inch balls; place 2 inches apart on an ungreased baking sheet. Flatten cookies with bottom of a glass dipped in 2 tablespoons flour. In a small bowl, mix remaining 1/4 cup butter, remaining 4 tablespoons flour, and syrup; stir until well blended. Spoon chocolate mixture into a pastry bag fitted with a small round tip. Pipe tree design onto each cookie. Bake 8 to 10 minutes or until edges are lightly browned. Transfer to a wire rack to cool completely. Store in an airtight container.

Yield: about 6 dozen cookies

CHOCOLATE MINT-TOPPED COOKIES

3/4 cup butter or margarine, softened
3/4 cup sugar
1 egg
4 teaspoons milk
1 teaspoon vanilla extract
1/2 teaspoon almond extract
2 cups all-purpose flour
1 1/2 teaspoons baking powder
1/4 teaspoon salt
1 package (12 ounces) individually wrapped layered chocolate mints
  Green candied cherry halves to decorate

In a large bowl, cream butter and sugar until fluffy. Add egg, milk, and extracts; beat until smooth. In a small bowl, combine flour, baking powder, and salt. Add dry ingredients to creamed mixture; stir until a soft dough forms. Shape dough into a ball. Wrap in plastic wrap and chill 1 hour.

Preheat oven to 375 degrees. On a lightly floured surface, use a floured rolling pin to roll out dough to 1/8-inch thickness. Use a 2 1/4-inch-diameter fluted-edge cookie cutter to cut out cookies. Transfer to a greased baking sheet. Bake 7 to 9 minutes or until bottoms are lightly browned. Remove from oven and immediately place 1 mint on top of each hot cookie; allow to soften. Spread softened mint evenly over each cookie. Decorate each cookie with a cherry half. Transfer to a wire rack to cool completely. Store in an airtight container.
Yield: about 4 dozen cookies

CHINESE NEW YEAR COOKIES

1/2 cup butter or margarine, softened
1 cup sugar
2 eggs
1/2 teaspoon vanilla extract
2 1/4 cups all-purpose flour
2 teaspoons baking powder
1 teaspoon Chinese five-spice powder
1 teaspoon finely chopped crystallized ginger
1/4 teaspoon salt

Preheat oven to 375 degrees. In a large bowl, cream butter and sugar until fluffy. Add eggs and vanilla; beat until smooth. In a medium bowl, combine flour, baking powder, Chinese five-spice powder, crystallized ginger, and salt. Add dry ingredients to creamed mixture; stir until a soft dough forms. On a lightly floured surface, use a floured rolling pin to roll out dough to 1/8-inch thickness. Use a 3-inch-wide animal-shaped cookie cutter (for current Chinese New Year) to cut out cookies. Transfer to an ungreased baking sheet. Bake 8 to 10 minutes or until edges are lightly browned. Transfer to a wire rack to cool completely. Store in an airtight container.
Yield: about 4 dozen cookies

PEPPERMINT SNOWBALLS

1 1/4 cups crushed peppermint candies (about 45 round candies)
1 1/3 cups sugar, divided
1/2 cup butter or margarine, softened
1/4 cup vegetable shortening
2 eggs
1 teaspoon peppermint extract
3/4 teaspoon vanilla extract
2 1/2 cups all-purpose flour
1/4 teaspoon salt

Preheat oven to 350 degrees. In a food processor, finely grind peppermint candies and 1/3 cup sugar to a powdery consistency; transfer to a small bowl. In a large bowl, cream butter, shortening, and remaining 1 cup sugar until fluffy. Add eggs and extracts; beat until smooth. In a medium bowl, combine flour and salt. Add dry ingredients to creamed mixture; stir until a soft dough forms. Shape dough into 1-inch balls. Roll balls in candy mixture. For best results, place 6 cookies at a time on an ungreased baking sheet. Bake 8 minutes; immediately roll hot cookies in candy mixture. Transfer to a wire rack to cool completely. Repeat with remaining dough. Store in an airtight container.
Yield: about 5 1/2 dozen cookies

Made with crystallized ginger and pungent Chinese five-spice powder, crispy Chinese New Year Cookies (clockwise from top left) are a taste-tempting treat. Cool Peppermint Snowballs are rolled in a mixture of crushed peppermints and sugar. Soft and chewy, Chocolate Mint-Topped Cookies pair almond-accented cookies with a chocolate-mint icing.

CHRISTMAS TREE COOKIES

1 cup butter or margarine,
   softened
1 cup sugar
2 eggs
1 teaspoon vanilla extract
3 1/3 cups all-purpose flour
1 teaspoon baking powder
1/2 teaspoon salt
1 cup finely crushed hard red
   candies (about 20 candies)

In a large bowl, cream butter and sugar until fluffy. Add eggs and vanilla; beat until smooth. In a medium bowl, combine flour, baking powder, and salt. Add dry ingredients to creamed mixture; stir until a soft dough forms. Wrap in plastic wrap and chill 1 hour.

Preheat oven to 350 degrees. On a lightly floured surface, use a floured rolling pin to roll out dough to 1/8-inch thickness. Use a 4 1/2-inch tree-shaped cookie cutter to cut out cookies. Transfer to a lightly greased aluminum foil-lined baking sheet. Use a heart-shaped aspic cutter to cut heart from center of each cookie. Bake 8 to 10 minutes or until cookies are firm. Cool completely on pan; leave cookies on foil to decorate.

In a small saucepan, melt candies over medium heat; reduce heat to low. Spoon melted candies into each heart cutout. Allow candies to harden. Carefully remove cookies from foil. Store in an airtight container.
Yield: about 5 1/2 dozen cookies

RUSSIAN ROCK COOKIES

1 cup butter or margarine,
   softened
1 cup granulated sugar
1/2 cup firmly packed brown sugar
1/2 cup light corn syrup
1/2 cup buttermilk
3 eggs, beaten
1 teaspoon vanilla extract
3 1/4 cups all-purpose flour, divided
1 package (8 ounces) chopped
   dates
1 tablespoon ground cinnamon
1 teaspoon ground cloves
1 teaspoon ground nutmeg
1/2 teaspoon baking soda
1/4 teaspoon salt
1 jar (10 ounces) maraschino
   cherries, drained and chopped
2 cups chopped pecans

Preheat oven to 350 degrees. In a large bowl, cream butter and sugars until fluffy. Add corn syrup, buttermilk, eggs, and vanilla; beat until smooth. In a small bowl, combine 1/4 cup flour and dates; stir until dates are coated with flour. In a medium bowl, combine remaining 3 cups flour, cinnamon, cloves, nutmeg, baking soda, and salt. Add dry ingredients to creamed mixture; stir until a soft dough forms. Stir in dates, cherries, and pecans. Drop teaspoonfuls of dough 1 inch apart onto a greased baking sheet. Bake 12 to 15 minutes or until edges are lightly browned. Transfer to a wire rack to cool completely. Store in an airtight container.
Yield: about 8 dozen cookies

ORANGE-MOLASSES CRISPIES

1/3 cup butter or margarine,
   softened
1/2 cup vegetable shortening
3/4 cup sugar
1/4 cup molasses
2 tablespoons orange-flavored
   liqueur
2 teaspoons grated orange zest
1/2 teaspoon vanilla extract
1 1/2 cups all-purpose flour
1 teaspoon baking soda
1 cup finely chopped walnuts

Preheat oven to 350 degrees. In a large bowl, cream butter, shortening, and sugar until fluffy. Stir in molasses, orange liqueur, orange zest, and vanilla until well blended. In a small bowl, combine flour and baking soda. Add dry ingredients to creamed mixture; stir until a soft dough forms. Stir in walnuts. Drop teaspoonfuls of dough 1 inch apart onto a greased baking sheet. Bake 8 to 10 minutes or until cookies are golden brown. Allow cookies to cool on pan 3 minutes; transfer to a wire rack to cool completely. Store in an airtight container.
Yield: about 5 dozen cookies

Dates, maraschino cherries, and pecans add pizzazz to cake-like Russian Rock Cookies (clockwise from top left). Perfect as an accompaniment to coffee or tea, Orange-Molasses Crispies will be a hit with those who enjoy brickly cookies. Christmas Tree Cookies have heart-shaped cutouts with a sweet filling of melted hard candies.

Create your own visions of sugarplums by making picture-perfect Cherry Sugarplums! These delicacies feature candied cherries wrapped in creamy cherry-flavored fondant and drenched in luscious dark chocolate.

CHERRY SUGARPLUMS

1/3 cup butter, softened
1/3 cup light corn syrup
1 teaspoon cherry flavoring
  Liquid red food coloring
4 cups sifted confectioners sugar
1 container (4 ounces) red candied cherries, halved
6 ounces chocolate candy coating
4 ounces bittersweet baking chocolate

In a medium bowl, cream butter and corn syrup until fluffy. Stir in cherry

flavoring; tint pink. Beating with an electric mixer, gradually add confectioners sugar to butter mixture until too stiff to beat. Stir in remaining sugar. Pour mixture onto a dampened smooth surface. Knead until very smooth and creamy. Using teaspoonfuls of candy mixture, shape balls around cherry halves. Place balls on waxed paper. Lightly cover with waxed paper and allow to dry overnight at room temperature.

In a heavy medium saucepan over low heat, melt candy coating and bittersweet chocolate. Remove chocolate from heat. Placing each ball on a fork and holding over saucepan, spoon chocolate over balls. Place balls on a baking sheet covered with waxed paper. Place in refrigerator to allow chocolate to harden. Store in an airtight container in a cool place.
Yield: about 5 1/2 dozen candies

16

Beautifully decorated with icing and food coloring, each of our Santa Cookies is a little work of art. The buttery cookies are shaped in a cookie mold.

SANTA COOKIES

COOKIES
1 cup butter or margarine, softened
1 cup firmly packed brown sugar
1/2 cup granulated sugar
1 egg
1 teaspoon vanilla extract
3 1/2 cups all-purpose flour
1 teaspoon ground coriander
1/4 teaspoon salt

ICING
6 tablespoons sifted confectioners sugar
4 teaspoons milk
  Burgundy, green, and black paste food coloring

Preheat oven to 350 degrees. For cookies, cream butter and sugars in a medium bowl until fluffy. Add egg and vanilla; beat until smooth. In a small bowl, combine flour, coriander, and salt. Add dry ingredients to creamed mixture; stir until a soft dough forms. Press small pieces of dough into a greased and lightly floured cookie mold. Use a sharp knife to loosen edges of dough. Invert mold onto a greased baking sheet. Tap edge of mold lightly to release dough. Repeat for remaining dough. Bake 10 to 12 minutes or until edges of cookies are brown. Transfer to a wire rack to cool completely.

For icing, combine sugar and milk until smooth. To decorate cookies, dilute each food coloring with a small amount of water. Referring to photo, use a paintbrush to paint food coloring on each cookie. Use a clean paintbrush to brush white icing on each cookie for beard, mustache, eyebrows, and trim on coat, hat, and sled. Brush icing lightly over each sled. Allow icing to harden. Store in an airtight container.
Yield: about 1 dozen 5-inch cookies

MINIATURE TOFFEE CHEESECAKES

CRUST
- 1/2 cup butter or margarine, softened
- 1/2 cup firmly packed brown sugar
- 1 teaspoon vanilla extract
- 1 1/4 cups all-purpose flour
- 1/2 cup finely chopped pecans

FILLING
- 2 packages (8 ounces each) cream cheese, softened
- 1/2 cup firmly packed brown sugar
- 2 eggs
- 1 teaspoon vanilla-butter-nut flavoring
- 1 package (6 ounces) milk chocolate-covered toffee bits

For crust, cream butter, brown sugar, and vanilla in a medium bowl until fluffy. Add flour; stir until well blended. Stir in pecans. Press 1 teaspoon crust mixture into bottom of each paper-lined cup of a miniature muffin pan.

Preheat oven to 350 degrees. For filling, beat cream cheese and brown sugar in a medium bowl until fluffy. Add eggs and vanilla-butter-nut flavoring; beat until well blended. Stir in toffee bits. Spoon 1 tablespoon filling mixture over each crust. Bake 16 to 18 minutes or until filling is set in center. Place pan on a wire rack to cool. Store in refrigerator in an airtight container.

Yield: about 5 dozen miniature cheesecakes

PEPPERMINT DIVINITY

- 1 jar (7 ounces) marshmallow creme
- 2 cups sugar
- 1/2 cup water
- 2 tablespoons light corn syrup
- 1/8 teaspoon salt
- 1/2 teaspoon vanilla extract
- 3/4 cup finely crushed peppermint candies (about 6 ounces)

Spoon marshmallow creme into a large heatproof bowl; set aside. Butter sides of a heavy medium saucepan. Combine sugar, water, corn syrup, and salt in saucepan. Stirring constantly, cook over medium heat until sugar dissolves. Using a pastry brush dipped in hot water, wash down any sugar crystals on sides of pan. Attach a candy thermometer to pan, making sure thermometer does not touch bottom of pan. Increase heat to medium-high and bring to a boil. Cook, without stirring, until syrup reaches hard-ball stage (approximately 250 to 268 degrees). Test about 1/2 teaspoon syrup in ice water. Syrup will roll into a hard ball in ice water and will remain hard when removed from the water. Remove from heat. While beating with an electric mixer on medium speed, slowly pour syrup over marshmallow creme. Add vanilla and increase speed of mixer to high. Continue to beat about 3 minutes or just until mixture holds its shape. Quickly stir in crushed candies. Press into a greased 8-inch square pan. Allow to harden. Cut into 1-inch squares. Store in an airtight container.

Yield: about 4 dozen candies

HOLLY MINTS

- 4 1/2 cups sifted confectioners sugar
- 5 tablespoons butter, softened
- 3 tablespoons evaporated milk
- 12 drops peppermint-flavored oil
  Green liquid food coloring
  Small red cinnamon candies to garnish

In a large bowl, combine confectioners sugar, butter, evaporated milk, and flavored oil; tint green. Knead mixture until smooth and color is well blended. Firmly press mixture into a 1 1/2-inch-long rubber leaf-shaped candy mold. Immediately remove from mold and place on waxed paper. Garnish mints with cinnamon candies for holly berries. Store in a cool place in a container with a loose-fitting lid.

Yield: about 9 dozen mints

Crushed peppermint candies give a refreshing flavor to an old favorite. Cut into squares, our Peppermint Divinity (left, on plate) is simply divine! Miniature Toffee Cheesecakes are yummy bite-size morsels. Sweet, dainty Holly Mints have cinnamon candy "berries."

With their sprinkling of confectioners sugar, our flaky Christmas Rosettes (clockwise from lower left) resemble snow-covered Christmas trees. Mint leaves are stirred into the batter of Fresh Mint Cookies for a light, delicious treat. Chock-full of chopped walnuts and candied cherries, Cherry-Walnut Fudge is a colorful Yuletide sweet.

CHERRY-WALNUT FUDGE

2¹/4 cups sugar
¹/2 cup sour cream
¹/4 cup milk
2 tablespoons butter or margarine
1 tablespoon light corn syrup
¹/4 teaspoon salt
2 teaspoons vanilla extract
1 cup coarsely chopped walnuts
¹/2 cup candied cherries, quartered

Line a 7 x 11-inch baking pan with aluminum foil, extending foil over ends of pan. Grease foil and set pan aside. Butter sides of a heavy large saucepan. Combine sugar, sour cream, milk, butter, corn syrup, and salt. Stirring constantly, cook over medium-low heat until sugar dissolves. Using a pastry brush dipped in hot water, wash down any sugar crystals on sides of pan. Attach a candy thermometer to pan, making sure thermometer does not touch bottom of pan. Increase heat to medium and bring to a boil. Cook, without stirring, until syrup reaches soft-ball stage (approximately 234 to 240 degrees). Test about ¹/2 teaspoon syrup in ice water. Syrup will easily form a ball in ice water but will flatten when held in your hand. Place pan in 2 inches of cold water in sink. Add vanilla; do not stir. Cool to approximately 110 degrees. Using medium speed of an electric mixer, beat fudge until thickened and no longer glossy. Stir in walnuts and cherries. Spread mixture into prepared pan. Cool completely. Use ends of foil to lift fudge from pan. Cut into 1-inch squares. Store in an airtight container in a cool place.
Yield: about 5 dozen pieces fudge

CHRISTMAS ROSETTES

³/4 cup evaporated milk
2 eggs
2 teaspoons vanilla extract
1 cup sifted all-purpose flour
2 tablespoons granulated sugar
¹/8 teaspoon salt
Vegetable oil
Sifted confectioners sugar

In a medium bowl, combine evaporated milk, eggs, and vanilla; whisk until well blended. In a small bowl, combine flour, granulated sugar, and salt. Gradually add dry ingredients to milk mixture; whisk until smooth. Cover and chill mixture 30 minutes.

Place ³/4 inch of oil in a heavy medium saucepan over medium-high heat. Preheat rosette iron in hot oil. Remove iron from heat and blot on paper towel. For each rosette, dip bottom of iron into batter and

immediately into hot oil. Batter should release from iron. If not, gently shake iron to release batter. Cook about 30 seconds or until lightly browned; drain on paper towels. Sprinkle warm rosettes with confectioners sugar. Store in a single layer between sheets of waxed paper in an airtight container.
Yield: about 8 dozen rosettes

FRESH MINT COOKIES

Prepare dough one day in advance to allow flavors to blend.

1 1/2   cups butter or margarine, softened
2/3   cup superfine granulated sugar
1   egg
2   tablespoons minced fresh mint leaves
1   tablespoon grated orange zest
1/2   teaspoon vanilla extract
2   cups all-purpose flour
    Granulated sugar

In a large bowl, cream butter and superfine sugar until fluffy. Add egg, mint leaves, orange zest, and vanilla; beat until smooth. Add flour to creamed mixture; stir until a soft dough forms. Cover dough and chill overnight.

Preheat oven to 350 degrees. Shape dough into 1-inch balls. Place balls 1 inch apart on an ungreased baking sheet; flatten balls with bottom of a glass dipped in granulated sugar. Bake 7 to 9 minutes or until edges are lightly browned. Transfer cookies to a wire rack to cool. Store in an airtight container.
Yield: about 6 dozen cookies

CINNAMON-WALNUT BISCOTTI

2   cups all-purpose flour
1   cup plus 2 tablespoons sugar, divided
1/2   teaspoon baking soda
1/2   teaspoon baking powder
1/4   teaspoon salt
2   eggs
1   egg yolk
1   teaspoon vanilla extract

A touch of orange adds extra zip to Cinnamon-Walnut Biscotti. Topped with sugar and cinnamon, these delightful coffee-dunkers are extra crunchy because they're baked twice — once as a loaf and again as slices.

1   tablespoon grated orange zest
1 1/2   cups coarsely chopped walnuts, toasted
1/4   teaspoon ground cinnamon
1   egg
1   teaspoon water

Preheat oven to 300 degrees. Using an electric mixer with a dough hook attachment, combine flour, 1 cup sugar, baking soda, baking powder, and salt in a large bowl until well blended. In a small bowl, whisk 2 eggs, 1 egg yolk, vanilla, and orange zest. Add egg mixture to flour mixture; continue beating until a soft dough forms. Turn onto a lightly floured surface. Add walnuts and knead 3 minutes or until walnuts are evenly distributed. Divide dough in half. On a greased and floured baking sheet, shape each piece of dough into a 2 1/2 x 10-inch loaf, flouring hands as necessary. Allow 3 inches between loaves on baking sheet. In a small bowl, combine remaining 2 tablespoons sugar and cinnamon. In another small bowl, beat 1 egg and water. Brush loaves with egg mixture; sprinkle with sugar and cinnamon mixture. Bake 45 to 50 minutes or until loaves are lightly browned; cool 10 minutes on baking sheet. Cut loaves diagonally into 1/2-inch slices. Lay cut cookies flat on a baking sheet. Bake 15 minutes, turn cookies over, and bake 15 minutes longer. Transfer cookies to a wire rack to cool completely. Store in an airtight container.
Yield: about 2 1/2 dozen cookies

BRANDIED FRUIT COOKIES

- 2 packages (8 ounces each) chopped dates
- 1 cup raisins
- ³/₄ cup brandy
- ³/₄ cup butter or margarine, softened
- 1 cup sugar
- ¹/₄ cup hot water
- 1 teaspoon baking soda
- 2 eggs
- 2 cups all-purpose flour
- 1 teaspoon ground cloves
- 4 cups chopped pecans
- 1 cup candied cherries, coarsely chopped
- 1 cup candied pineapple, coarsely chopped

Preheat oven to 350 degrees. In a large bowl, combine dates, raisins, and brandy; set aside.

In another large bowl, cream butter and sugar until fluffy. In a small bowl, combine hot water and baking soda. Add baking soda mixture and eggs to butter mixture; beat until smooth. In a small bowl, combine flour and cloves. Add dry ingredients to creamed mixture; stir until a soft dough forms. Stir in brandied fruit mixture, pecans, cherries, and pineapple. Drop teaspoonfuls of dough 2 inches apart onto a greased baking sheet. Bake 9 to 11 minutes or until edges are lightly browned. Transfer cookies to a wire rack to cool. Store in a single layer between sheets of waxed paper in an airtight container.

Yield: about 8 dozen cookies

NUTTY CARAMELS

- 2 cups sugar
- 2 cups whipping cream, divided
- 1¹/₂ cups light corn syrup
- ³/₄ cup butter
- 1¹/₂ cups finely chopped pecans, toasted
- 1 teaspoon vanilla extract

Butter sides of a heavy Dutch oven. Combine sugar, 1 cup whipping cream, corn syrup, and butter in pan.

Nutty Caramels (left) *are chewy tidbits loaded with toasted pecans. Brandied Fruit Cookies have all the appeal of traditional fruitcake — with a little added punch.*

Stirring constantly, cook over medium-low heat until sugar dissolves. Using a pastry brush dipped in hot water, wash down any sugar crystals on sides of pan. Attach a candy thermometer to pan, making sure thermometer does not touch bottom of pan. Continuing to stir, increase heat to medium and bring to a boil. Gradually add remaining 1 cup whipping cream. Stirring frequently without touching sides of pan, cook until syrup reaches firm-ball stage (approximately 242 to 248 degrees).

Test about ¹/₂ teaspoon syrup in ice water. Syrup will roll into a firm ball in ice water but will flatten if pressed when removed from water. Remove from heat and stir in pecans and vanilla. Immediately pour into a buttered 10¹/₂ x 15¹/₂-inch jellyroll pan. Cool at room temperature several hours. Cut into 1-inch squares using a lightly oiled heavy knife. Wrap each candy piece in a foil candy wrapper and store in a cool place.

Yield: about 12¹/₂ dozen caramels

MOCHA-NUT FUDGE

 4   cups sugar
 1/2   teaspoon salt
 1   cup evaporated milk
 1/3   cup light corn syrup
 6   tablespoons butter, divided
 1/2   cup coffee-flavored liqueur
 2   teaspoons vanilla extract
 1 1/2   cups semisweet chocolate
       chips, melted
 1   cup finely chopped toasted
       pecans

Butter sides of a heavy large saucepan. Combine sugar and salt in saucepan. Add evaporated milk, corn syrup, and 3 tablespoons butter. Stirring constantly, cook over medium-low heat until sugar dissolves. Using a pastry brush dipped in hot water, wash down any sugar crystals on sides of pan. Attach a candy thermometer to pan, making sure thermometer does not touch bottom of pan. Increase heat to medium and bring to a boil. Cook, without stirring, until syrup reaches soft-ball stage (approximately 234 to 240 degrees). Test about 1/2 teaspoon syrup in ice water. Syrup will easily form a ball in ice water but will flatten when held in your hand. Remove from heat. Add remaining 3 tablespoons butter, liqueur, and vanilla; do not stir. Place pan in 2 inches of cold water in sink. Cool to approximately 110 degrees. Add melted chocolate. Using medium speed of an electric mixer, beat until thickened and no longer glossy. Stir in pecans. Drop teaspoonfuls of mixture onto waxed paper. Cool completely. Store in an airtight container in a cool place.
Yield: about 8 dozen pieces fudge

LEMON-PECAN COOKIES

 1/2   cup butter or margarine, softened
 1/4   cup vegetable shortening
 1   cup sugar
 1   egg
 2   tablespoons honey
 1   teaspoon grated lemon zest
 1/2   teaspoon lemon extract
 2   cups all-purpose flour

Laced with coffee-flavored liqueur and crunchy pecans, Mocha-Nut Fudge (left) is a chocolate lover's delight! Lemon-Pecan Cookies combine the tangy taste of lemon and the buttery richness of pecans to create tummy-tempting yummies.

 1/2   teaspoon baking soda
 1/2   teaspoon cream of tartar
 1/4   teaspoon salt
 1   cup finely chopped toasted
       pecans

Preheat oven to 375 degrees. In a large bowl, cream butter, shortening, and sugar until fluffy. Add egg, honey, lemon zest, and lemon extract; beat until smooth. In a small bowl, combine flour, baking soda, cream of tartar, and salt. Add dry ingredients to creamed mixture; stir until a soft dough forms. Stir in pecans. Drop tablespoonfuls of dough 3 inches apart onto a lightly greased baking sheet. Bake 6 to 8 minutes or until bottoms are lightly browned. Transfer cookies to a wire rack to cool. Store in an airtight container.
Yield: about 3 1/2 dozen cookies

TURTLE BROWNIES
(Shown on page 24)

BROWNIES
 1   cup butter or margarine
 4   ounces unsweetened baking
       chocolate
 4   eggs
 2   cups sugar
 1   teaspoon vanilla-butter-nut
       flavoring
 1 1/2   cups all-purpose flour
 1/2   teaspoon salt

TOPPING
 1   package (14 ounces) caramels
 2   tablespoons milk
 1 1/2   cups finely chopped toasted
       walnuts
 1   package (6 ounces) semisweet
       chocolate chips
 2   teaspoons vegetable shortening

Preheat oven to 350 degrees. For brownies, melt butter and chocolate in

Continued on page 24

Three layers of gooey goodness, Turtle Brownies (recipe on page 23) feature a dark brownie "crust" smothered in caramel and toasted walnuts with a topping of semisweet chocolate. Using only a few basic ingredients, you can make our cinnamon- and spearmint-flavored Stained Glass Candy. A light powdering of confectioners sugar gives the "glass" candy a frosted appearance.

top of a double boiler over simmering water; remove from heat and allow to cool. In a large bowl, lightly beat eggs. Add sugar and vanilla-butter-nut flavoring to eggs; beat until smooth. Combine chocolate mixture with sugar mixture. In a small bowl, combine flour and salt. Add dry ingredients to chocolate mixture; stir until smooth. Spread batter into a greased and floured 9 x 13-inch baking pan. Bake 25 to 30 minutes or until set in center. Place pan on a wire rack to cool.

For topping, place caramels and milk in top of a double boiler over medium heat. Stir until caramels melt. Stir in walnuts. Spoon caramel mixture over warm brownies, spreading evenly. Allow brownies to cool. In a small microwave-safe bowl, microwave chocolate chips on high power (100%) 2 minutes, stirring after each

minute. Add shortening; stir until well blended. Spread over caramel topping. Allow chocolate to harden. Cut into 1¹/₂-inch squares. Store in an airtight container.
Yield: about 3 dozen brownies

STAINED GLASS CANDY

    1   cup sifted confectioners sugar
3³/₄   cups granulated sugar
1¹/₄   cups light corn syrup
    1   cup water
 ¹/₈   teaspoon **each** spearmint-
        and cinnamon-flavored oils
        Green and red liquid food
        coloring

Spread confectioners sugar evenly into two 10¹/₂ x 15¹/₂-inch jellyroll pans. In a heavy large saucepan, combine granulated sugar, corn syrup,

and water. Stirring constantly, cook over medium-low heat until sugar dissolves. Using a pastry brush dipped in hot water, wash down any sugar crystals on sides of pan. Attach a candy thermometer to pan, making sure thermometer does not touch bottom of pan. Increase heat to medium-high and bring to a boil. Cook, without stirring, until syrup reaches soft-crack stage (approximately 270 to 290 degrees). Test about ¹/₂ teaspoon syrup in ice water. Syrup will form hard threads in ice water but will soften when removed from the water. Remove from heat; immediately pour half of syrup into a second heated saucepan. Add spearmint oil and green food coloring to half of syrup; add cinnamon oil and red food coloring to remaining syrup. Pour each flavored candy into separate jellyroll pans. Allow candy to cool completely; break into pieces. Store in an airtight container.
Yield: about 2 pounds candy

WINTER FOREST CHRISTMAS TREES

COOKIES
    1   cup butter or margarine, softened
1¹/₂   cups sifted confectioners sugar
    1   egg
1¹/₂   teaspoons vanilla extract
2¹/₂   cups all-purpose flour
 ¹/₂   teaspoon baking soda
 ¹/₄   teaspoon cream of tartar

DECORATING ICING
3¹/₂   cups sifted confectioners sugar
 ¹/₃   cup milk
 ³/₄   teaspoon liquid green food
        coloring
 ¹/₂   teaspoon mint extract
        White coarse decorating sugar
        to decorate

ROYAL ICING
 ¹/₂   cup sifted confectioners sugar
2¹/₄   teaspoons water
    1   teaspoon meringue powder
        Yellow and red paste food
        coloring

For cookies, cream butter and confectioners sugar in a large bowl until fluffy. Add egg and vanilla; beat until smooth. In a medium bowl, combine flour, baking soda, and cream of tartar. Add dry ingredients to creamed mixture; stir until a soft dough forms. Divide dough in half. Wrap in plastic wrap and chill 3 hours.

Preheat oven to 375 degrees. On a lightly floured surface, use a floured rolling pin to roll out half of dough to 1/8-inch thickness. Use a 3 x 5 1/4-inch tree-shaped cookie cutter to cut out cookies. Transfer cookies to a lightly greased baking sheet. Bake 5 to 7 minutes or until bottoms are lightly browned. Transfer to a wire rack with waxed paper underneath to cool. Repeat with remaining dough.

For decorating icing, combine confectioners sugar, milk, food coloring, and mint extract in a medium bowl; stir until smooth. Ice cookies. Before icing is completely dry, sprinkle with coarse decorating sugar. Allow icing to harden.

For royal icing, beat confectioners sugar, water, and meringue powder in a small bowl with an electric mixer 7 to 10 minutes or until stiff. Place 2 tablespoons icing in a small bowl; tint yellow. Tint remaining icing red. Spoon red icing into a pastry bag fitted with a medium round tip. Pipe red birds onto trees. Spoon yellow icing into a pastry bag fitted with a very small round tip. Pipe small beaks onto birds. Allow icing to harden.

Store in single layers between sheets of waxed paper in an airtight container.
Yield: about 2 dozen cookies

BUTTER-PECAN BRITTLE

    2 cups sugar
  3/4 cup light corn syrup
  1/4 cup water
    3 cups coarsely chopped toasted
          pecans
  1/4 cup butter
    1 teaspoon vanilla extract
  1/2 teaspoon salt
    1 teaspoon baking soda

Winter Forest Christmas Trees (top) *are tasty, attractive treats festively crowned with minty green icing, tiny frosting cardinals, and a sprinkling of coarse sugar. Butter-Pecan Brittle is packed with nuts for delicious snacking during the holiday season.*

Butter sides of a heavy large saucepan. Combine sugar, corn syrup, and water in saucepan. Stirring constantly, cook over medium-low heat until sugar dissolves. Using a pastry brush dipped in hot water, wash down any sugar crystals on sides of pan. Attach a candy thermometer to pan, making sure thermometer does not touch bottom of pan. Increase heat to medium and bring to a boil. Cook, without stirring, until syrup reaches hard-crack stage (approximately 300 to 310 degrees) and turns light golden in color. Test about 1/2 teaspoon syrup in ice water. Syrup will form brittle threads in ice water and will remain brittle when removed from the water. Remove from heat and stir in pecans, butter, vanilla, and salt; stir until butter melts. Add baking soda (syrup will foam); stir until soda dissolves. Pour syrup onto a large piece of buttered aluminum foil. Using a buttered spatula, pull edges of warm candy until stretched thin. Cool completely. Break into pieces. Store in an airtight container.
Yield: about 2 pounds brittle

Chunky Chocolate-Caramel Chewies (lower right) are a nutty delight. A dusting of confectioners sugar adds sweetness to light Butter-Nut Cookies. Striped with vanilla candy coating, Chocolate Squares have a hint of almond flavor.

CHOCOLATE SQUARES

1/2 cup butter or margarine, softened
1 cup sugar
1/3 cup (about 4 ounces) almond paste
2 eggs
1 teaspoon vanilla extract
1 teaspoon chocolate extract
1 3/4 cups all-purpose flour
3/4 cup cocoa
1 teaspoon baking powder
1/4 teaspoon salt
4 ounces vanilla candy coating

In a medium bowl, cream butter and sugar until fluffy. Add almond paste, eggs, and extracts. Beat 2 minutes at high speed of an electric mixer. In a small bowl, combine flour, cocoa, baking powder, and salt. Add dry ingredients to creamed mixture; stir until a soft dough forms. Shape dough into 2 balls. Wrap in plastic wrap and chill 1 hour.

Preheat oven to 350 degrees. On a lightly floured surface, use a floured rolling pin to roll out each half of dough to 1/4-inch thickness. Using a sharp knife, cut dough into 2-inch squares. Transfer to a greased baking sheet. Bake 10 to 12 minutes or until firm. Transfer to a wire rack to cool completely.

In a small saucepan, melt candy coating over low heat, stirring constantly. Spoon candy coating into a pastry bag fitted with a medium round tip. Pipe stripes on cookies. Allow coating to harden. Store in an airtight container.

Yield: about 4 dozen cookies

BUTTER-NUT COOKIES

- 1 cup butter or margarine, softened
- 1 1/2 cups sifted confectioners sugar, divided
- 1 teaspoon vanilla-butter-nut flavoring
- 2 cups all-purpose flour
- 1/4 teaspoon salt
- 3/4 cup coarsely ground pecans, toasted

Preheat oven to 375 degrees. In a large bowl, cream butter, 3/4 cup confectioners sugar, and vanilla-butter-nut flavoring until fluffy. In a small bowl, combine flour and salt. Add dry ingredients and pecans to creamed mixture; stir until well blended. Shape dough into 1-inch balls; place on an ungreased baking sheet. Bake 12 to 14 minutes or until firm to touch and bottoms are lightly browned. When cool enough to handle, roll in remaining 3/4 cup confectioners sugar. Transfer cookies to waxed paper; allow to cool completely. Roll in confectioners sugar again. Store in an airtight container.

Yield: about 5 1/2 dozen cookies

CHOCOLATE-CARAMEL CHEWIES

- 3/4 cup butter or margarine, softened
- 1/2 cup firmly packed brown sugar
- 2 eggs
- 1 teaspoon vanilla extract
- 1 1/2 cups all-purpose flour
- 1/4 teaspoon baking soda
- 1/4 teaspoon salt
- 1 1/2 cups chopped pecans
- 1 cup milk chocolate chips
- 22 caramel candies, quartered

Preheat oven to 350 degrees. In a medium bowl, cream butter and brown sugar until fluffy. Add eggs and vanilla; stir until smooth. In a small bowl, combine flour, baking soda, and salt. Add dry ingredients to creamed mixture; stir until a soft dough forms. Stir in pecans, chocolate chips, and caramel pieces. Drop tablespoonfuls of dough 2 inches apart onto a greased

Crushed corn flakes and chopped nuts give Crunchy Pecan Cookies their munchiness.

baking sheet. Bake 8 to 10 minutes or until edges are lightly browned. Allow cookies to cool slightly on pan; transfer to a wire rack to cool completely. Store in an airtight container.

Yield: about 4 dozen cookies

CRUNCHY PECAN COOKIES

- 1 cup butter or margarine, softened
- 1 cup granulated sugar
- 1 cup firmly packed brown sugar
- 1 cup vegetable oil
- 1 egg
- 1 teaspoon vanilla extract
- 3 1/2 cups all-purpose flour
- 1 teaspoon baking soda
- 1/2 teaspoon salt
- 2 cups finely crushed corn flake cereal
- 1 1/2 cups chopped pecans

Preheat oven to 350 degrees. In a large bowl, cream butter and sugars until fluffy. Beat in oil, egg, and vanilla. In a medium bowl, combine flour, baking soda, and salt. Add dry ingredients to creamed mixture; stir until a soft dough forms. Stir in cereal crumbs and pecans. Drop tablespoonfuls of dough 2 inches apart onto a greased baking sheet. Using a fork dipped in water, make a crisscross design on each cookie. Bake 10 to 12 minutes or until edges are light brown. Transfer to a wire rack to cool completely. Store in an airtight container.

Yield: about 7 dozen cookies

Crunchy Party Mix has a yummy cinnamon-sugar coating. This super-easy snack mix is loaded with your favorite nibbles, such as candy-coated chocolate pieces, raisins, and roasted peanuts.

CRUNCHY PARTY MIX

- 2 cups small pretzels
- 2 cups chow mein noodles
- 2 cups square corn cereal
- 1 cup lightly salted roasted peanuts
- 1 cup raisins
- 3 egg whites
- 1 1/2 cups sugar
- 1 teaspoon ground cinnamon
- 1 teaspoon salt
- 1 package (14 ounces) candy-coated chocolate pieces

Preheat oven to 225 degrees. In a very large bowl, combine pretzels, chow mein noodles, cereal, peanuts, and raisins.

In a medium bowl, beat egg whites until foamy. Stir in sugar, cinnamon, and salt. Pour over pretzel mixture; stir until well coated. Spread evenly on a greased baking sheet. Bake 1 hour, stirring every 15 minutes. Cool completely on pan. Stir in chocolate pieces. Store in an airtight container.
Yield: about 12 cups snack mix

CHOCOLATE-RASPBERRY SQUARES

- 1 cup butter or margarine, softened
- 1 1/2 cups sugar, divided
- 2 egg yolks
- 2 1/2 cups all-purpose flour
- 1 jar (12 ounces) raspberry jelly
- 1 cup semisweet chocolate mini chips
- 4 egg whites
- 1/4 teaspoon salt
- 2 cups coarsely ground hazelnuts

Preheat oven to 350 degrees. In a medium bowl, cream butter and 1/2 cup sugar until fluffy. Add egg yolks to butter mixture; beat until smooth. Stir in flour until well blended. Press dough into bottom of a greased 10 x 15-inch jellyroll pan. Bake 15 to 20 minutes or until lightly browned. Spread jelly over hot crust; sprinkle chocolate chips over jelly. Beat egg whites until foamy. Gradually add remaining 1 cup sugar and salt; beat until stiff peaks form. Fold in hazelnuts. Gently spread egg white mixture over chocolate layer. Bake 20 to 25 minutes or until lightly browned on top. Cool completely in pan. Cut into 2-inch squares. Store in an airtight container.

Yield: about 3 dozen squares

CHRISTMAS ORNAMENT COOKIES

COOKIES

- 3/4 cup butter or margarine, softened
- 1/2 cup granulated sugar
- 1 egg
- 1 teaspoon vanilla extract
- 1 3/4 cups all-purpose flour
- 3 tablespoons cornstarch
- 1/2 teaspoon baking powder
- 1/8 teaspoon salt
- 2 tablespoons confectioners sugar

FILLING

- 2 tablespoons butter or margarine, softened
- 2 tablespoons vegetable shortening
- 3/4 cup sifted confectioners sugar
- 2 teaspoons milk
- 3/4 teaspoon peppermint extract
- 1/2 teaspoon **each** red and green powdered food coloring

Preheat oven to 350 degrees. For cookies, cream butter and granulated sugar in a medium bowl until fluffy. Add egg and vanilla; beat until smooth. In a small bowl, combine flour, cornstarch, baking powder, and salt. Add flour mixture to creamed mixture; stir until a soft dough forms. On a lightly floured surface, use a floured rolling pin to roll out dough to 1/8-inch thickness. Use a 3-inch-diameter fluted-edge cookie cutter to cut out cookies. Transfer to a greased baking sheet. Use a 2-inch star-shaped cookie cutter to cut out centers of half of cookies on baking sheet. Bake 10 to 12 minutes or until edges are lightly browned. Transfer to a wire rack with waxed paper underneath to cool completely. Sift confectioners sugar over warm star cutout cookies.

As pretty as holiday jewels, Christmas Ornament Cookies (right) get four stars for their buttery taste and creamy peppermint filling. Chewy Chocolate-Raspberry Squares are capped with a nutty meringue-like topping.

For filling, cream butter, shortening, and confectioners sugar in a medium bowl until well blended. Stir in milk and peppermint extract. Divide filling into 2 small bowls; tint red and green.

Spread a thin layer of filling on top of each whole cookie and place a star cutout cookie on top. Allow filling to harden. Store in an airtight container.

Yield: about 20 cookies

29

HOLIDAY OPEN HOUSE

*D*uring this season of joy, we delight in opening our homes to share good times, good food, and good cheer with the special people in our lives. This year, impress your guests with choice selections from our collection of party favorites. From tasty finger foods and yummy spreads to delicious drinks and tempting desserts, you can select dishes to ensure a great time for all. Whether your festivities are formal or casual, our palate-pleasing dishes will set the tone for a memory-making occasion.

Delectable Pizza Bites (recipe on page 32) are zippy delights! Topped with lots of fresh veggies, Canadian bacon, and feta cheese, these flavorful snacks add Italian flair to the buffet.

PIZZA BITES (Shown on pages 30 and 31)

DOUGH

- 1 package dry yeast
- 1 cup warm water
- 1 teaspoon sugar
- 2 tablespoons vegetable oil
- 1 teaspoon salt
- 2 1/2 cups all-purpose flour, divided
  Vegetable cooking spray

TOPPINGS

- 5 plum tomatoes, thinly sliced and divided
- 1 sweet yellow pepper, thinly sliced
- 1 to 2 ounces feta cheese, crumbled
- 1 to 2 cloves garlic, minced
- 1 teaspoon dried basil leaves
- 4 tablespoons olive oil, divided
- 2 ounces Canadian bacon, cut into bite-size pieces
- 1 sweet red pepper, thinly sliced
- 1 green pepper, thinly sliced
- 1 small onion, thinly sliced and separated into rings
- 1 can (2 1/4 ounces) sliced black olives, drained
- 2 tablespoons finely chopped fresh cilantro **or** 2 teaspoons dried cilantro
- 1/2 teaspoon ground cumin
- 1 cup (4 ounces) shredded mozzarella cheese

For dough, dissolve yeast in warm water in a medium bowl. Add sugar, oil, salt, and 2 cups flour; stir until a soft dough forms. Turn onto a lightly floured surface; adding remaining 1/2 cup flour, knead 5 minutes or until dough becomes smooth and elastic. Place in a medium bowl sprayed with cooking spray, turning once to coat top of dough. Cover and let rise in a warm place (80 to 85 degrees) 1 hour or until doubled in size.

Preheat oven to 400 degrees. Using half of dough, shape into eight 1 1/2-inch balls. On a lightly floured surface, use a floured rolling pin to roll out each ball into a 5-inch circle. Transfer dough circles to an ungreased baking sheet.

For toppings, place half of tomato slices on dough circles. Layer yellow pepper, feta cheese, garlic, and basil over tomato slices; drizzle 2 tablespoons olive oil evenly over toppings. Repeat procedure with remaining dough, layering with remaining tomato slices, Canadian bacon, red and green peppers, onion rings, black olives, cilantro, cumin, and mozzarella cheese. Drizzle with remaining 2 tablespoons olive oil. Bake 20 to 25 minutes. Cut each pizza into 4 wedges; serve warm.
Yield: 64 pizza bites

CHRISTMAS CHEESE STAR

- 2 1/2 cups (10 ounces) shredded sharp Cheddar cheese
- 1 container (12 ounces) cottage cheese
- 1 package (8 ounces) cream cheese, softened
- 1 jar (4 ounces) diced pimientos, drained
- 2 tablespoons dried minced onion
- 1/2 teaspoon garlic powder
- 1/2 teaspoon ground red pepper
  Sweet red pepper, cucumber, and parsley to garnish
  Crackers to serve

Line a 1-quart star-shaped mold with plastic wrap. In a large bowl, combine cheeses, pimientos, onion, garlic powder, and ground red pepper using an electric mixer. Spoon into prepared mold. Cover and chill 1 hour. Invert mold onto a serving plate. Remove plastic wrap. Cover and refrigerate until ready to serve.

To serve, let stand at room temperature 20 to 30 minutes or until softened. Use a small star-shaped aspic cutter to cut stars from sweet red pepper. Garnish cheese star with cucumber slices, red pepper stars, and parsley. Serve with crackers or bread.
Yield: about 3 3/4 cups cheese spread

Lightly spiced with red pepper and garlic, our Christmas Cheese Star has a festive garnish of sweet red pepper, cucumber, and fresh parsley. This creamy spread, molded in a traditional holiday shape, is an eye-catching accent for the Yuletide table.

For a zesty snack that takes just minutes to make, quick-fry hearty Tortilla Chips and serve with make-ahead South of the Border Salsa.

MEXICAN CHOCOLATE BROWNIES

  1 cup cocoa
  3/4 cup butter or margarine, melted
  1 1/4 cups all-purpose flour
  1/2 teaspoon salt
  3 cups sugar
  7 eggs, lightly beaten
  1 tablespoon vanilla extract
  2 1/2 teaspoons ground cinnamon
  1 teaspoon freshly ground black
      pepper

Preheat oven to 350 degrees. In a small bowl, combine cocoa with butter, stirring until smooth. In a large bowl, combine flour, salt, and sugar. Stir in cocoa mixture, eggs, vanilla, cinnamon, and pepper. Pour into a lightly greased 9 x 13 x 2-inch baking pan and bake 35 to 40 minutes or until center is set.
Yield: about 2 dozen brownies

ZESTY TOMATO JUICE

  1 can (48 ounces) tomato juice
  1/2 cup lemon juice
  1/4 cup Worcestershire sauce
  2 tablespoons juice from canned
      or bottled jalapeño peppers
  1 1/2 teaspoons hot pepper sauce
  1/2 teaspoon onion juice

Combine tomato juice, lemon juice, Worcestershire sauce, pepper juice, pepper sauce, and onion juice; stir well. Store in refrigerator.
Yield: about 6 servings

NACHO CHEESE SNACK MIX

  6 cups rice cereal squares
  4 cups cheese snack sticks
  2 cups small pretzels
  2 cups mixed nuts
  1/2 cup butter, melted
  1 tablespoon Worcestershire
      sauce
  1 package (1 1/4 ounces) cheese
      sauce mix
  2 teaspoons chili powder
  1/4 teaspoon ground red pepper

SOUTH OF THE BORDER SALSA

Keep this salsa and a package of tortillas in the refrigerator to serve drop-in guests.

  1 can (28 ounces) whole
      tomatoes with liquid, chopped
  1/2 cup olive oil
  1/2 cup minced fresh parsley
  1 medium onion, minced
  1/4 cup chopped jalapeño peppers
  2 cloves garlic, minced
      Tortilla Chips to serve

Combine tomatoes, olive oil, parsley, onion, peppers, and garlic in a non-metallic container. Refrigerate overnight to allow flavors to blend. Serve with Tortilla Chips.
Yield: about 3 cups salsa

TORTILLA CHIPS

  1 package (12 count) fresh corn
      tortillas
      Vegetable oil
  1 tablespoon salt
  1 clove garlic, minced

Cut each tortilla into 6 wedges. Pour oil into a skillet to a depth of 1 inch. Heat oil to 360 degrees over medium-high heat. Fry tortillas, a few at a time, about 1 minute or until crisp. Drain on paper towels. Place salt and garlic in a plastic bag. Add chips and shake well. Serve warm or at room temperature.
Yield: 6 dozen chips

Pep up your holiday with a Mexican fiesta! (Clockwise from top left) Nibblers will love Nacho Cheese Snack Mix, which packs a chili powder pick-me-up. Other easy-to-make dishes include Zesty Tomato Juice with peppery pizzazz, Mexican Chocolate Brownies flavored with cinnamon, and Spicy Jalapeño Spread, a blend of shredded Cheddar and chopped vegetables.

Preheat oven to 250 degrees. Combine cereal, cheese sticks, pretzels, and nuts in a large roasting pan. In a small bowl, combine melted butter, Worcestershire sauce, cheese sauce mix, chili powder, and red pepper. Pour over cereal mixture; stir until well coated. Bake 30 minutes, stirring every 10 minutes. Spread on waxed paper to cool. Store in an airtight container.
Yield: 14 cups snack mix

SPICY JALAPEÑO SPREAD

4 cups (16 ounces) shredded sharp Cheddar cheese
1 cup mayonnaise
1 medium white onion, finely chopped
1/2 cup chopped green onions
6 jalapeño peppers, chopped
2 cloves garlic, minced
1 teaspoon garlic salt
Crackers to serve

In a large bowl, combine cheese, mayonnaise, white onion, green onions, peppers, garlic, and garlic salt; stir until well blended. Refrigerate overnight to allow flavors to blend before serving. Serve with crackers.
Yield: about 4 1/2 cups spread

36

CHERRY-MOCHA WARMER

- 2 cups very hot strongly brewed coffee **or** 2 cups boiling water and 2 tablespoons instant coffee granules
- 4 ounces semisweet baking chocolate, chopped
- 2/3 cup granulated sugar
- 1/8 teaspoon salt
- 4 cups half and half
- 2 cups milk
- 3/4 cup crème de cacao
- 3/4 cup cherry brandy
- 1 cup whipping cream
- 1/4 cup sifted confectioners sugar Maraschino cherries with stems to garnish

Chill a small bowl and beaters from an electric mixer in freezer. In a double boiler over hot water, combine coffee, chocolate, granulated sugar, and salt. Whisk until chocolate is melted and smooth. In a medium saucepan, scald half and half and milk; whisk into chocolate mixture. Whisk in crème de cacao and brandy. Keep chocolate mixture warm.

In chilled bowl, beat whipping cream until soft peaks form. Gradually add confectioners sugar and beat until stiff peaks form. Serve each warm beverage with a dollop of whipped cream and a maraschino cherry.

Yield: about fourteen 6-ounce servings

Pepper and Olive Crostini feature a marinated mixture of roasted red and green peppers, stuffed green olives, and tangy capers on slices of crispy French bread. Cherry Tomatoes Stuffed with Basil Cheese are delicious little bites, and spirited Cherry-Mocha Warmer is laced with crème de cacao and cherry brandy.

PEPPER AND OLIVE CROSTINI

- 2 large green peppers
- 2 large sweet red peppers
- 1 jar (5 ounces) stuffed green olives, drained and sliced
- 2 tablespoons minced red onion
- 1 tablespoon drained capers
- 6 tablespoons olive oil, divided
- 1 tablespoon balsamic vinegar
- 1/4 cup butter
- 1 clove garlic, minced
- 2 loaves 2 1/2-inch-diameter French bread, sliced into 1/2-inch slices

To roast peppers, cut in half lengthwise and remove seeds and membranes. Place, skin side up, on an ungreased baking sheet; flatten with hand. Broil about 3 inches from heat about 15 to 20 minutes or until peppers are blackened and charred. Immediately seal peppers in a plastic bag and allow to steam 10 to 15 minutes. Remove charred skin. Cut peppers into thin 2 1/2-inch-long strips. Combine peppers, olives, onion, capers, 2 tablespoons olive oil, and vinegar in a medium bowl.

Preheat oven to 300 degrees. In a small saucepan over medium-low heat, combine remaining 4 tablespoons olive oil, butter, and garlic; heat about 7 minutes. Brush butter mixture on both sides of French bread slices and place on an ungreased baking sheet. Bake 10 to 12 minutes or until light golden and crisp. Spread pepper mixture over warm bread slices and serve immediately.

Yield: about 44 appetizers

CHERRY TOMATOES STUFFED WITH BASIL CHEESE

- 20 cherry tomatoes
- 1/2 cup part-skim ricotta cheese
- 2 tablespoons freshly grated Parmesan cheese
- 1 tablespoon chopped fresh basil **or** 1/2 teaspoon dried basil leaves
- 1 small clove garlic, minced
- 1/8 teaspoon crushed red pepper flakes
- 1/8 teaspoon salt
- 1/8 teaspoon ground black pepper

Cut a small slice from bottom of each tomato. Cut around stem of each tomato and use a small melon baller to scoop out pulp; invert in a colander to drain.

In a food processor, combine ricotta cheese, Parmesan cheese, basil, garlic, red pepper flakes, salt, and black pepper; process until well blended. Place cheese mixture in a pastry bag fitted with a large star tip; pipe cheese mixture into each tomato. Store in an airtight container in refrigerator. Serve chilled.

Yield: 20 tomatoes

MUSHROOMS IN CREAM CHEESE PASTRY

2 1/2   cups all-purpose flour
 3/4   teaspoon salt, divided
   2   packages (8 ounces each) cream cheese, softened
 3/4   cup butter or margarine, softened
  12   ounces fresh mushrooms, quartered
 1/2   cup freshly grated Parmesan cheese
   2   tablespoons dry white wine
   2   tablespoons chopped fresh parsley
   2   tablespoons chopped pimiento
   1   clove garlic, minced
   1   teaspoon dried marjoram leaves
 1/8   teaspoon ground white pepper
 1/8   teaspoon dry mustard
   1   egg, beaten

In a medium bowl, combine flour and 1/2 teaspoon salt. Using a pastry blender or 2 knives, cut in cream cheese and butter until mixture resembles coarse meal. Lightly knead dough. Divide dough in half and wrap in plastic wrap; chill 1 hour.

In a food processor, process mushrooms, Parmesan cheese, wine, parsley, pimiento, garlic, marjoram leaves, remaining 1/4 teaspoon salt, white pepper, and dry mustard until coarsely chopped. Allow mushroom mixture to stand 15 minutes; drain in a colander.

Preheat oven to 400 degrees. On a lightly floured surface, use a floured rolling pin to roll out half of dough to 1/8-inch thickness. Use a 3-inch-diameter fluted-edge cookie cutter to cut out dough. For each dough circle, place a scant teaspoon of mushroom filling on half of circle; brush edge of remaining half of circle with beaten egg. Fold dough over filling. Use a floured fork to crimp edges of dough together and to prick top of pastry. Place on an ungreased baking sheet. Bake 15 to 20 minutes or until lightly browned. Serve warm.

Mushrooms in Cream Cheese Pastry (top) *have a filling of fresh mushrooms and Parmesan cheese nestled in a rich crust. Made with red peppers and green chiles, Cheesy Pepper Rice Squares are smothered with two kinds of cheese.*

Unbaked pastries may be placed on a baking sheet and frozen. Store frozen pastries in an airtight container. Bake frozen pastries 20 to 25 minutes in a preheated 400-degree oven.
Yield: about 5 dozen pastries

CHEESY PEPPER RICE SQUARES

   4   cups cooked white rice
1 1/2   cups (6 ounces) shredded Monterey Jack cheese, divided
1 1/2   cups (6 ounces) shredded Cheddar cheese, divided
   1   cup sour cream

Awaken the table with Festive Shrimp Appetizer! Highlighted with holiday colors, the shrimp and vegetables are tossed in a zesty oil and vinegar mixture.

2 cans (4 ounces each) whole green chiles, drained
1 jar (7 ounces) roasted red peppers, drained

Preheat oven to 325 degrees. In a medium bowl, combine rice, 1 cup Monterey Jack cheese, 1 cup Cheddar cheese, and sour cream until well blended. Firmly press half of rice mixture into bottom of a greased 7 x 11-inch baking pan. Cut green chiles open; place over rice mixture. Press remaining rice mixture over green chiles. Place roasted red peppers over rice mixture. Bake uncovered 25 to 30 minutes; sprinkle remaining cheese over red peppers. Bake 5 minutes longer or until cheese melts. Place pan on a wire rack and allow to cool 15 minutes. Cut into 2-inch squares. Serve warm.
Yield: about 15 servings

FESTIVE SHRIMP APPETIZER

2 pounds medium shrimp, cooked, peeled, and deveined
1 medium white onion, cut into bite-size pieces
1 large sweet red pepper, cut into bite-size pieces
1 large green pepper, cut into bite-size pieces

1 jar (5 ounces) stuffed green olives, drained
1/2 cup olive oil
1/4 cup white rice vinegar
3/4 teaspoon red peppercorns
1/2 teaspoon green peppercorns

In a large bowl, combine shrimp, onion, red and green peppers, olives, olive oil, vinegar, and peppercorns; lightly toss until well coated. Cover and refrigerate overnight to allow flavors to blend. Serve chilled.
Yield: about 7 cups shrimp

OYSTERS CREOLE IN PEPPERED PASTRY SHELLS

Fresh oysters are cooked with lots of chopped vegetables and seasoned the way they are down South.

 4 jars (10 ounces each) fresh oysters, drained, reserving liquor
1/3 cup butter
 1 cup finely chopped celery
 1 cup finely chopped fresh parsley
1/2 cup finely chopped onion
1/2 cup finely chopped green onions
 1 cup finely chopped green pepper
 1 cup cracker crumbs
1/2 teaspoon salt
3/4 teaspoon Cajun seasoning
1/2 teaspoon ground black pepper
1/4 teaspoon ground red pepper
 2 eggs, beaten
1 1/2 tablespoons Worcestershire sauce
 5 tablespoons ketchup
    Peppered Pastry Shells (recipe follows)

Chop oysters and set aside. In a large skillet, melt butter and add vegetables; sauté until tender. Add 1/2 cup reserved oyster liquor to vegetables and cook slowly until all liquid has evaporated. While vegetables are cooking, blend cracker crumbs with remaining oyster liquor; set aside.

In a saucepan, combine vegetables, crumbs, salt, Cajun seasoning, black pepper, and red pepper. Add eggs; blend well. Cook over low heat for 25 minutes. Add oysters, Worcestershire sauce, and ketchup. Cook 5 more minutes. Serve hot in Peppered Pastry Shells.
Yield: 25 servings

PEPPERED PASTRY SHELLS
 1 package (3 ounces) cream cheese, softened
1/2 cup butter, softened
 1 cup all-purpose flour
1/2 teaspoon ground white pepper

An authentic Cajun country recipe, Oysters Creole features a medley of tender, spicy chopped vegetables cooked with oysters. The delightful dish is served hot in Peppered Pastry Shells.

In a small bowl, blend cream cheese and butter. Combine flour and white pepper; add to cheese mixture. Blend mixture with a fork until a ball forms. Cover with waxed paper and chill for 2 hours.

Preheat oven to 425 degrees. On a lightly floured surface, roll out dough to 1/8-inch thickness. Cut out dough with a 3-inch round pastry cutter. Press dough into 1 1/2 to 2 1/2-inch fluted tart pans. Trim any excess dough with a sharp knife. Prick bottom of dough with a fork. Place tarts on a baking sheet. Bake 10 to 12 minutes. Turn out of pans and cool completely on wire racks. Store in airtight containers or freeze until ready to use.
Yield: 30 to 32 shells

SMOKED OYSTER ROLL
 2 packages (8 ounces each) cream cheese, softened
2 1/2 tablespoons mayonnaise
 2 teaspoons Worcestershire sauce
 2 garlic cloves, pressed
 1 tablespoon finely minced onion
 2 cans (3 3/4 ounces each) smoked oysters, drained and chopped
    Crackers to serve

In a medium bowl, beat cream cheese, mayonnaise, Worcestershire sauce, garlic, and onion until smooth.
On a large sheet of foil, spread mixture into a 12 x 19-inch rectangle (about 1/2-inch thick). Place in

Your guests will come back for more of these scrumptious hors d'oeuvres! The yummy trio of party treats includes easy-to-prepare Party Cheese Rolls (from left), butter-flavored Burgundy Mushrooms, and tasty Smoked Oyster Roll wrapped in savory cream cheese.

refrigerator until mixture begins to set.

Remove from refrigerator and spread oysters on top of mixture. Beginning at 1 long side, gently roll up mixture. Wrap tightly and chill for 24 hours.

Transfer to a serving plate and serve with crackers.

Yield: 12 to 14 servings

BURGUNDY MUSHROOMS

These delicious mushrooms are simmered all day. They can be frozen in small containers and heated when friends drop in.

1 1/2 cups butter
1 quart red wine (a medium-priced Burgundy is best)
2 tablespoons Worcestershire sauce
1 teaspoon dill seed
1 teaspoon ground black pepper
1 teaspoon garlic powder
2 cups boiling water
3 beef bouillon cubes

3 chicken bouillon cubes
4 pounds fresh mushrooms
Salt

In a large Dutch oven, combine butter, wine, Worcestershire sauce, dill seed, pepper, garlic powder, water, and bouillon; bring to a boil.

Clean mushrooms with a damp paper towel and trim ends of stems. Add mushrooms to liquid and reduce heat to simmer. Cover and cook 5 to 6 hours. Remove lid and cook 4 more hours. When ready, liquid should just cover mushrooms. Salt to taste. Serve hot.

Yield: 12 to 16 servings

PARTY CHEESE ROLLS

Make several recipes and freeze.

5 dozen small finger rolls (about 2 1/2 inches long)
2 cups (8 ounces) shredded sharp Cheddar cheese

2 cups (8 ounces) shredded mild Cheddar cheese
1 can (4 1/2 ounces) ripe olives, chopped
6 hard-cooked eggs, chopped
1 can (4 ounces) green chiles, chopped
1 cup tomato sauce
1 teaspoon celery salt
1 medium onion, finely chopped
1 cup butter, softened

Preheat oven to 400 degrees. Split rolls in half. Using a small spoon, scoop out centers of rolls; reserve half of the crumbs. In a large bowl, combine remaining ingredients; add reserved crumbs. Stuff rolls with mixture. Bake 10 to 15 minutes. Serve immediately.

To make ahead, unbaked rolls can be placed in an airtight container and frozen. To bake after freezing, thaw completely, wrap in foil, and heat.

Yield: 60 rolls

HAM PINWHEELS

1 package (8 ounces) cream cheese, softened
1/4 cup chopped black olives
2 tablespoons chopped toasted almonds
2 tablespoons mayonnaise
2 tablespoons chopped green onion
1 tablespoon sherry
1 teaspoon dry mustard
1/2 teaspoon paprika
1/4 teaspoon salt
1/4 teaspoon freshly ground black pepper
1/8 teaspoon ground red pepper
3 to 4 drops hot pepper sauce
5 rectangular slices (about 5 ounces) baked ham

Beat cream cheese until smooth. Stir in olives, almonds, mayonnaise, green onion, sherry, dry mustard, paprika, salt, black pepper, red pepper, and pepper sauce. Spread mixture on ham slices. Beginning at 1 long edge, roll up ham slices jellyroll style. Place, seam side down, on baking sheet. Freeze 30 minutes. Remove from freezer and slice each roll into about 8 pieces. Insert a toothpick through each slice.
Yield: about 40 pinwheels

MINI HOT BROWNS

3 tablespoons butter or margarine
3 tablespoons all-purpose flour
1/2 cup shredded sharp Cheddar cheese
1 cup milk
1/2 teaspoon salt
1/2 teaspoon ground white pepper
1 1/2 cups finely diced cooked turkey breast
8 slices bacon, cooked and crumbled
20 slices thinly sliced white bread
3/4 cup freshly grated Parmesan cheese

In a medium saucepan, melt butter over medium-low heat. Whisk in flour, blending well. Add Cheddar cheese, whisking constantly until smooth.

These cheesy appetizers will certainly be the hit of the party! (Clockwise from top) *Greek Potato Skins are topped with feta cheese and herbs. Mini Hot Browns feature a creamy mixture of turkey, bacon, and Cheddar. Ham Pinwheels are good-tasting roll-ups accented with crunchy almonds and a touch of hot pepper sauce.*

Increase heat to medium. Whisking constantly, slowly add milk; cook 4 to 5 minutes or until sauce is thick and smooth. Remove from heat and stir in salt, white pepper, turkey, and bacon; set aside.

Preheat broiler. Trim crusts from bread and cut each slice into four squares. Place bread on baking sheets and toast 1 side under broiler.

Spread a heaping tablespoon of turkey mixture on untoasted side of each piece of bread. Place on baking sheets. Sprinkle with Parmesan cheese. Broil a few seconds or until cheese melts and mixture begins to bubble. Serve warm.
Yield: 80 appetizers

GREEK POTATO SKINS

3 medium baking potatoes, scrubbed
Olive oil

4 ounces feta cheese, crumbled
1 1/2 teaspoons dried oregano leaves
1/2 teaspoon dried basil leaves
1/4 teaspoon dried rosemary leaves
1/2 teaspoon garlic salt

Preheat oven to 400 degrees. Prick potatoes and rub with oil. Bake potatoes 1 hour or until done.

Cool potatoes slightly. Preheat oven to 450 degrees. Cut potatoes in half lengthwise. Leaving about a 1/4-inch shell, scoop out pulp (reserve pulp for another use, if desired). Cut skins in half lengthwise again; then cut skins in half crosswise. Place skins on a baking sheet and brush generously with oil. Bake 5 minutes. Combine remaining ingredients. Remove skins from oven and top with cheese mixture. Drizzle with more oil. Broil 2 to 3 minutes or until cheese is bubbly.
Yield: 24 potato skins

OATMEAL BREAD WREATHS

 2 packages dry yeast
 1/3 cup warm water
 2 cups water
 1 cup old-fashioned rolled oats
 6 cups all-purpose flour
 1/2 cup nonfat dry milk
 2 1/2 teaspoons salt
 1/3 cup molasses
 1/4 cup vegetable oil
  Vegetable cooking spray

In a small bowl, dissolve yeast in 1/3 cup warm water. In a medium saucepan, bring 2 cups water to a boil. Remove from heat; stir in oats. Cool to room temperature.

In a large bowl, combine flour, dry milk, and salt. Add oat mixture, yeast mixture, molasses, and oil to dry ingredients. Stir until a soft dough forms. Turn onto a lightly floured surface and knead until dough becomes smooth and elastic. Place in a large bowl sprayed with cooking spray, turning once to coat top of dough. Cover and let rise in a warm place (80 to 85 degrees) 1 hour or until doubled in size. Turn dough onto a lightly floured surface and punch down. Divide dough into thirds. Shape each piece of dough into a ball, make a hole in center of dough, and place in a greased 9-inch tube pan. Spray top of dough with cooking spray, cover, and let rise in a warm place 1 hour or until doubled in size.

Preheat oven to 350 degrees. Bake 25 to 30 minutes or until bread sounds hollow when tapped. Remove from pans and cool completely on a wire rack. Store in an airtight container.
Yield: 3 loaves bread

HOAGIE SANDWICH

 1 Oatmeal Bread Wreath
  Mayonnaise and/or mustard
  Lettuce
 1/2 pound thinly sliced cooked ham
 1/2 pound thinly sliced cooked smoked turkey
 6 ounces thinly sliced Cheddar cheese

Mint leaves and red pepper "berries" make a festive garnish on our Oatmeal Bread Wreath. Sliced and filled with layers of cold cuts and cheese, the wreath becomes a Hoagie Sandwich with Yuletide flair.

  Sliced tomatoes
  Sweet red pepper
  Fresh mint leaves

Cut loaf of bread in half horizontally. If desired, spread mayonnaise and/or mustard over each half of bread. Layer lettuce, ham, turkey, cheese, and tomatoes on bottom half of bread.

Replace top of bread. Use an aspic cutter to cut small round pieces of red pepper. Use a small amount of mayonnaise or mustard to secure mint leaves and red pepper pieces to top of sandwich to resemble holly leaves and berries. Cover and refrigerate until ready to serve.
Yield: 10 to 12 servings

Creamy Shrimp Spread (top) is delicious served with crackers. Topped with red pepper and provolone cheese, Sausage-Cream Cheese Squares have a delightful flaky crust prepared with refrigerated crescent roll dough.

SHRIMP SPREAD

Shrimp spread should be made 1 day in advance.

1½ pounds cooked, peeled, and deveined shrimp
1 package (8 ounces) cream cheese, softened
¼ cup finely chopped onion
2 tablespoons sour cream
2 teaspoons sweet pickle relish
1½ teaspoons Dijon-style mustard
1½ teaspoons hot pepper sauce
Crackers or bread to serve

Reserve several shrimp for garnish. Finely chop remaining shrimp. In a large bowl, combine chopped shrimp, cream cheese, onion, sour cream, pickle relish, mustard, and hot pepper sauce; stir until well blended. Cover and refrigerate 8 hours or overnight to allow flavors to blend.

To serve, garnish with reserved shrimp. Serve with crackers or bread.
Yield: about 4 cups spread

SAUSAGE-CREAM CHEESE SQUARES

2 cans (8 ounces each) refrigerated crescent rolls
2 packages (8 ounces each) cream cheese, softened
½ teaspoon dried basil leaves, crushed
¼ teaspoon garlic powder
1½ pounds mild pork sausage, cooked, drained, and crumbled
12 ounces provolone cheese, shredded (about 3 cups)
¾ cup finely chopped sweet red pepper

Preheat oven to 350 degrees. Unroll 1 can of crescent roll dough into 2 long rectangles. Place on a greased baking sheet. With long sides touching, form an 8 x 13-inch rectangle, pressing edges to seal. Repeat for remaining can of rolls, using a second greased baking sheet. Bake 12 to 15 minutes or until golden brown. Remove from oven.

A zippy blend of three cheeses, green onions, and pepper sauce, flavorful Green Onion Cheese Balls are rolled in chili powder for a grand finish!

In a medium bowl, beat cream cheese, basil, and garlic powder using an electric mixer. Spread cream cheese mixture evenly over baked dough. Sprinkle sausage, provolone cheese, and sweet red pepper evenly over cream cheese mixture. Bake 5 to 7 minutes or until cheese melts. Cut into 2-inch squares and serve warm.
Yield: about 4 dozen appetizers

GREEN ONION CHEESE BALLS

2 cups (8 ounces) shredded sharp Cheddar cheese
2 cups (8 ounces) shredded Monterey Jack cheese
1 package (8 ounces) cream cheese, softened
1 cup finely chopped green onions
2 teaspoons hot pepper sauce
Chili powder
Crackers to serve

Combine cheeses, green onions, and pepper sauce in a large bowl. Beat with electric mixer until well blended. Shape cheese mixture into 3 balls. Roll in chili powder. Serve with crackers.
Yield: 3 cheese balls, about 1 cup each

CURRIED SNACK STICKS

- 1 can (16 ounces) salted peanuts
- 1 package (10 ounces) pretzel sticks
- 1 can (7 ounces) potato sticks
- 1/2 cup vegetable oil
- 1 package (1 1/4 ounces) white sauce mix
- 1 tablespoon curry powder
- 1/2 teaspoon ground red pepper
- 1/2 teaspoon ground cumin seed

Preheat oven to 300 degrees. In a large roasting pan, combine peanuts, pretzel sticks, and potato sticks. In a small bowl, combine oil, white sauce mix, curry powder, red pepper, and cumin seed until well blended. Pour sauce mixture over peanut mixture; stir until well coated. Bake 20 minutes, stirring after 10 minutes. Spread on aluminum foil to cool. Store in an airtight container.

Yield: about 14 cups snack mix

Fast, easy Curried Snack Sticks are an irresistibly crunchy mix coated with tangy spices.

Glazed with melted butterscotch chips and studded with peanuts, Nutty Butterscotch Popcorn is a gourmet snack for popcorn lovers. Holiday hostesses will appreciate this quick make-ahead treat.

NUTTY BUTTERSCOTCH POPCORN

- 1 package (12 ounces) butterscotch chips
- 16 cups unsalted popped popcorn
- 1 can (16 ounces) salted peanuts

Place butterscotch chips in a small microwave-safe bowl. Microwave on high power (100%) about 3 minutes, stirring every minute until chips are melted. Place popcorn and peanuts in a very large bowl. Pour melted chips over popcorn mixture; stir until well coated. Spread on greased aluminum foil; allow to cool. Store in an airtight container.

Yield: about 20 cups flavored popcorn

APPLE-CINNAMON WINE

1 bottle (750 ml) dry white wine
3 medium Granny Smith apples, peeled, cored, and finely chopped (about 4 1/2 cups)
1/2 cup sugar
1/2 teaspoon ground cinnamon

In a 2-quart container, combine wine, apples, sugar, and cinnamon; stir until sugar dissolves. Cover and refrigerate 1 month to allow flavors to blend.

Use cheesecloth to strain wine, reserving 1/2 cup apples for Apple-Cinnamon Cheese Ball if desired (recipe follows). Serve wine chilled.
Yield: about 3 cups wine

APPLE-CINNAMON CHEESE BALL

1 package (8 ounces) cream cheese, softened
1/2 cup apples from Apple-Cinnamon Wine
1/4 cup chopped pecans
1/4 teaspoon ground cinnamon
Chopped pecans
Sugar cookies to serve

In a medium bowl, combine cream cheese, apples, 1/4 cup pecans, and cinnamon. Shape into a ball and roll in pecans. Wrap cheese ball in plastic wrap and refrigerate 8 hours or overnight to allow flavors to blend.

To serve, let stand at room temperature 20 to 30 minutes or until softened. Serve with sugar cookies.
Yield: 1 cheese ball

What a combo! Apple-Cinnamon Wine has a mellow, fruity flavor. The Apple-Cinnamon Cheese Ball, made using fruit from the wine, is terrific with cookies or vanilla wafers.

The flaky pastry for savory Crab-Cream Cheese Bake (from left) is easily prepared with refrigerated crescent roll dough. Orange-Glazed Pecans are perfect for nibbling. Cheesy Snack Mix blends ranch-style dressing, garlic, and cheeses.

CRAB-CREAM CHEESE BAKE

1   package (8 ounces) cream
     cheese, softened
1/4 cup chopped green onions
1/2 teaspoon dried dill weed
1   can (8 ounces) refrigerated
     crescent rolls
1   can (6 1/2 ounces) crabmeat,
     drained
1   egg yolk, beaten

Preheat oven to 350 degrees. In a medium bowl, combine cream cheese, onions, and dill weed. Unroll crescent roll dough onto a greased baking sheet, being careful not to separate dough into pieces. Press dough into an 8 x 11-inch rectangle. Spoon crabmeat lengthwise along center of dough. Spoon cream cheese mixture over crabmeat. Fold long edges of dough over cream cheese mixture, slightly overlapping edges; pinch edges together to seal. Place, seam side down, on baking sheet. Lightly brush top of dough with egg yolk. Cut slits in top of dough. Bake 20 to 22 minutes or until golden brown and flaky. Cut into 1-inch slices and serve warm.
Yield: about 12 servings

CHEESY SNACK MIX

14 cups (about 20 ounces) small
     pretzels

1   cup butter or margarine
1   cup grated Parmesan cheese
3   packages (1 1/4 ounces each)
     cheese sauce mix
2   packages (1 ounce each)
     ranch-style salad dressing
     mix
1   teaspoon garlic powder

Preheat oven to 350 degrees. Place pretzels in a large bowl. In a medium saucepan, melt butter over medium heat. Remove from heat; stir in remaining ingredients. Pour over pretzels; stir until well coated. Transfer to 2 ungreased baking sheets. Bake 10 to 12 minutes or until golden brown. Cool completely on baking sheets. Store in an airtight container.
Yield: about 15 1/2 cups snack mix

ORANGE-GLAZED PECANS

- ¹/₂ cup granulated sugar
- ¹/₂ cup firmly packed brown sugar
- ¹/₂ cup sour cream
- 2 tablespoons frozen orange juice concentrate, thawed
- 1 teaspoon orange extract
- 3 cups unsalted pecan halves, toasted

In a medium saucepan, combine sugars, sour cream, and orange juice. Stirring constantly, cook over medium-low heat until sugars dissolve. Using a pastry brush dipped in hot water, wash down any sugar crystals on sides of pan. Attach candy thermometer to pan, making sure thermometer does not touch bottom of pan. Increase heat to medium and bring to a boil. Cook, without stirring, until syrup reaches soft-ball stage (approximately 234 to 240 degrees). Test about ¹/₂ teaspoon syrup in ice water. Syrup should easily form a ball in ice water but flatten when held in your hand. Remove from heat; stir in orange extract. Add pecans and stir until well coated. Spread pecan mixture on buttered aluminum foil. Allow to dry uncovered at room temperature 24 hours. Break apart and store in an airtight container.
Yield: about 4¹/₄ cups pecans

MACADAMIA CHEESE PUFFS

- 1 cup all-purpose baking mix
- 1 cup finely chopped unsalted macadamia nuts
- 1 cup (4 ounces) shredded Gruyère cheese
- ¹/₂ cup butter or margarine, softened
- 1 egg, beaten
- ¹/₂ teaspoon ground white pepper

Preheat oven to 375 degrees. In a medium bowl, combine baking mix, nuts, cheese, butter, egg, and white pepper; stir until a soft dough forms. Drop teaspoonfuls of dough onto a greased baking sheet. Bake 12 to

A yummy pop-in-your-mouth treat, Macadamia Cheese Puffs have the sweet, nutty taste of Gruyère cheese and the buttery richness of macadamias.

15 minutes or until edges are light brown. Cool on pan 2 minutes. Serve warm or transfer to a wire rack to cool completely. Store in an airtight container.
Yield: about 6 dozen cheese puffs

STUFFED SNOW PEAS

Stuffed snow peas may be prepared several hours ahead of time. Just wrap airtight and refrigerate until needed.

- 1/2 pound fresh snow peas
- 1 package (8 ounces) cream cheese, softened
- 2 tablespoons mayonnaise
- 1 teaspoon dried dill weed
- 1 teaspoon dried chives
- 1/2 teaspoon seasoned salt
- 1/2 teaspoon lemon pepper

Blanch snow peas in lightly salted boiling water 2 to 3 minutes. Drain and rinse in cold water to stop cooking.

In a medium bowl, combine cream cheese, mayonnaise, dill weed, chives, salt, and lemon pepper; beat until smooth. Using a sharp knife, split each snow pea open along straight edge. Place cheese mixture in a pastry bag fitted with a small star tip. Pipe cheese mixture inside each snow pea.
Yield: about 40 snow peas

SHRIMP TOAST

- 1/2 pound shrimp, peeled, deveined, and minced
- 6 canned water chestnuts, minced
- 1 tablespoon minced red onion
- 1 egg
- 1 tablespoon white wine
- 1 teaspoon ground ginger
- 1/2 teaspoon salt
- 1/8 teaspoon freshly ground black pepper
- 1 1/2 teaspoons cornstarch dissolved in 1 tablespoon water
- 6 slices day-old bread
   Vegetable oil for frying

In a small bowl, combine shrimp, water chestnuts, onion, egg, wine, ginger, salt, pepper, and cornstarch mixture, blending well. Trim crusts from bread. Spread shrimp mixture evenly onto bread. Cut each slice of bread in half diagonally. Cut in half again to form triangles.

Mushroom Paté (clockwise from lower left on plate) is a gourmet paté with creamy texture. Assemble Shrimp Toast ahead of time, then quick-fry just before serving. Dainty Stuffed Snow Peas have an herbed cheese filling. Black currant liqueur gives refreshing Kir Royale Punch (top) its pretty color.

In a skillet, heat 2 inches of oil to 360 degrees. Gently place bread, shrimp side up, in hot oil. Fry 1 minute, turn, and fry 15 seconds or until golden brown. Drain on paper towels. Serve immediately.
Yield: 24 toasts

MUSHROOM PATÉ

For full flavor, serve this simple paté at room temperature.

- 2/3 cup butter
- 2 pounds fresh mushrooms, finely chopped
- 1 teaspoon salt
- 1/2 teaspoon lemon pepper
- 1/2 teaspoon dried thyme leaves
- 3 egg yolks
- 1 tablespoon whipping cream or half and half
   French bread or crackers to serve

In a large skillet, melt butter over medium heat. Add mushrooms. Cook, stirring occasionally, until mushrooms are well browned and liquid cooks down (about 35 minutes). Stir in salt, lemon pepper, and thyme. Remove from heat.

In a small bowl, combine egg yolks with cream. Add 1/4 cup mushroom mixture to yolk mixture, stirring well. Combine yolk mixture with mushroom mixture in skillet. Stirring constantly, cook over low heat 3 minutes. Chill in an airtight container until firm. Serve at room temperature with crackers or French bread.
Yield: about 3 cups paté

KIR ROYALE PUNCH

1 bottle (750 ml) brut
    champagne, well chilled
1/4 cup crème de cassis liqueur

Combine champagne and liqueur in a quart container. Serve immediately.
Yield: about six 4-ounce servings

PEANUT BITES

1 loaf (1 pound) thinly sliced
    whole-wheat bread
2 cups smooth peanut butter
1/2 cup vegetable oil
3 tablespoons firmly packed
    brown sugar
1 1/2 cups honey-flavored wheat germ

Preheat oven to 250 degrees. Trim crusts from bread and discard. Cut each slice of bread in half diagonally; cut in half again to form triangles. Place triangles on an ungreased baking sheet. Bake 45 to 50 minutes or until light brown and dry.

In a medium saucepan, combine peanut butter, oil, and brown sugar over medium-low heat. Stir occasionally until heated through. Spread wheat germ on a large sheet of waxed paper. Add bread triangles to peanut butter mixture a few at a time, stirring carefully to coat triangles with mixture. Roll triangles in wheat germ. Place on wire racks to dry.
Yield: about 6 dozen bites

A grown-up treat featuring a childhood favorite, Peanut Bites (top) are crispy, not-too-sweet morsels. Coated with toasted pecans, Cream Cheese Grapes (recipe on page 52) are arranged in a cluster, then garnished with grapevine twigs and silk leaves.

CREAM CHEESE GRAPES

(Shown on page 51)

- 1 package (8 ounces) cream cheese, softened
- 2 tablespoons mayonnaise
- 1 pound seedless grapes
- 1½ cups finely chopped toasted pecans
  Artificial grapevine twigs and silk leaves to decorate

In a medium bowl, combine cream cheese and mayonnaise, beating until smooth. Add grapes to cream cheese and stir gently just until coated. Spread pecans on a large sheet of waxed paper. Roll the cheese-coated grapes in the pecans until well coated. Place grapes on a baking sheet and chill at least 1 hour. If desired, arrange on a serving platter in the shape of a grape cluster and decorate with grapevine twigs and silk leaves.

Yield: about 6 dozen grapes

HOT BACON-CHEESE DIP

- 3 rolls (6 ounces each) pasteurized process cheese food with garlic, quartered
- 2 cups sour cream
- 1 can (11½ ounces) bean and bacon soup
- 2 tablespoons dried chopped onion
- 2 teaspoons hot pepper sauce
- 2 teaspoons liquid smoke
- 2 teaspoons garlic powder
- 1 jar (2 ounces) real bacon pieces
  Chips to serve

Process cheese, sour cream, soup, onion, pepper sauce, liquid smoke, and garlic powder in a food processor until smooth. Transfer cheese mixture to a medium bowl; stir in bacon. Cover and refrigerate 8 hours or overnight to allow flavors to blend. Spoon dip into a large saucepan. Stirring occasionally, cook over medium heat until heated through. Serve warm with chips.

Yield: about 5 cups dip

Imperial Champagne Cocktails blend fruity drinks and champagne for an elegant apéritif. Hot pepper sauce and smoke flavoring add zest to Hot Bacon-Cheese Dip.

IMPERIAL CHAMPAGNE COCKTAILS

    2   cups tropical fruit punch drink
    2   cups orange juice
    1   cup peach schnapps
    1   bottle (750 ml) champagne,
          chilled

In a 2½-quart container, combine fruit punch, orange juice, and schnapps. Cover and refrigerate until well chilled.

To serve, stir in champagne. Serve chilled.

Yield: about ten 6-ounce servings

MARINATED MOZZARELLA

    1   pound mozzarella cheese, cut
          into thin 2-inch squares
   ¼   cup olive oil
    2   tablespoons finely chopped fresh
          parsley
    1   teaspoon garlic powder
    1   teaspoon onion powder
    1   teaspoon dried oregano leaves,
          crushed
   ¼   teaspoon ground black pepper
          Fresh basil leaves to garnish
          Bagel chips or crackers to serve

Place cheese in a single layer in a 10½ x 15½-inch jellyroll pan. In a small bowl, whisk oil, parsley, garlic powder, onion powder, oregano, and pepper. Pour over cheese. Cover and refrigerate 8 hours or overnight to allow flavors to blend, turning slices occasionally.

Arrange slices on a serving plate; garnish with fresh basil. Serve with bagel chips or crackers.

Yield: about 3 dozen cheese squares

Delicious with bagel chips or crackers, slices of Marinated Mozzarella get a mellow flavor from herbs and olive oil.

GRASSHOPPER PIE

CRUST
- 30 chocolate wafer cookies
- 1/4 cup butter or margarine, melted

FILLING
- 30 large marshmallows
- 1/2 cup milk
- 1/4 cup crème de menthe
- 1 cup whipping cream
  Green liquid food coloring (optional)
- 14 chocolate mint wafer candies to garnish

For crust, preheat oven to 350 degrees. In a food processor, finely grind cookies. With food processor running, slowly add melted butter; process until well blended. Press crumb mixture into bottom and up sides of a 9-inch pie pan. Bake crust 7 minutes. Cool completely on a wire rack.

For filling, place a medium bowl and beaters from an electric mixer in refrigerator until well chilled. In the top of a double boiler, combine marshmallows and milk. Stirring frequently, cook over hot, not boiling, water until smooth. Remove from heat and pour into a large bowl. Cool to room temperature. Stir in crème de menthe.

In chilled bowl, whip cream until soft peaks form. Fold whipped cream into marshmallow mixture. If desired, tint green. Spoon evenly into cooled crust. Loosely cover and refrigerate until set. Garnish with chocolate mint candies.
Yield: about 8 servings

CRANBERRY-CHAMPAGNE COCKTAILS

- 1 quart cranberry juice cocktail, chilled
- 1 bottle (750 ml) champagne, chilled

Combine cranberry juice and champagne in a 2-quart pitcher; stir until well blended. Serve chilled.
Yield: about nine 6-ounce servings

Accented with chocolate mint wafer candies, Grasshopper Pie combines a luscious crème de menthe filling with a tasty chocolate cookie crust. Festive Cranberry-Champagne Cocktails (not shown) are an elegant accompaniment to this dessert.

CHOCOLATE SNOWBALL COOKIES

1½ cups (9 ounces) semisweet chocolate chips
1 package (8 ounces) cream cheese, cut into small pieces
1½ teaspoons vanilla extract
3 cups finely ground chocolate wafer cookies (about 64 cookies)
1 cup finely ground pecans
Confectioners sugar, sifted

In a large saucepan, melt chocolate chips over low heat, stirring constantly. Add cream cheese and vanilla, stirring until smooth. Remove from heat. Stir in cookie crumbs and pecans. Shape into 1-inch balls; roll in confectioners sugar. Cover and refrigerate 8 hours or until firm.

Roll balls in confectioners sugar again. Store in an airtight container in refrigerator.

Yield: about 6 dozen cookies

CHOCOLATE EGGNOG

1 quart prepared eggnog
½ cup chocolate syrup
¼ teaspoon ground nutmeg
1 tablespoon vanilla extract
Ground nutmeg to garnish

In a large saucepan, combine eggnog, chocolate syrup, and ¼ teaspoon nutmeg. Stirring occasionally, cook over medium-low heat 20 to 25 minutes or until heated through (do not boil). Remove from heat; stir in vanilla. To serve, pour into cups; sprinkle lightly with nutmeg. Serve warm.

Yield: about six 6-ounce servings

A chocolate lover's version of the traditional Christmas beverage, Chocolate Eggnog is served warm with a garnish of ground nutmeg. Coated with confectioners sugar, picture-perfect Chocolate Snowball Cookies are delightful no-bake goodies.

FESTIVE FAMILY FEASTS

*S*pread holiday joy to the loved ones who surround your table this Christmas by serving taste-tempting dishes from our festive dinner collection. You can cook up a hearty stuffed ham, celebrate with an Olde English roast goose dinner, or carry your spirits south of the border for a holiday fiesta. We've also included recipes that are perfect for a neighborly progressive dinner and for making delicious use of day-old dishes. From a candlelit dinner to a Christmas Day buffet, your Yuletide feast will be an outstanding event when planned with our recipes in mind!

A flavorful stuffing makes moist Herb-Pecan Stuffed Turkey Breasts (recipe on page 60) a succulent alternative to traditional holiday turkey. Kissed with a hint of orange, tart and tangy Cranberry-Port Sauce (recipe on page 61) is the perfect condiment to serve with this entrée.

PARMESAN SPINACH AND ARTICHOKES

- ½ cup chopped green onions
- ½ cup chopped celery
- ½ cup butter or margarine
- 2 packages (10 ounces each) frozen chopped spinach, cooked and drained
- 2 cups sour cream
- 1 can (14 ounces) artichoke hearts, drained and chopped
- ½ teaspoon hot pepper sauce
- ½ teaspoon salt
- ¼ teaspoon ground black pepper
- 8 ounces bacon, cooked, crumbled, and divided
- ½ cup shredded Parmesan cheese

Preheat oven to 350 degrees. In a small saucepan over medium heat, cook onions and celery in butter until vegetables are tender. In a greased 2-quart baking dish, combine onion mixture, spinach, sour cream, artichoke hearts, pepper sauce, salt, and black pepper. Reserving 2 tablespoons bacon for garnish, stir remaining bacon into spinach mixture. Sprinkle cheese over top of casserole. Bake 30 to 40 minutes or until edges are lightly browned. Garnish with reserved bacon. Serve warm.
Yield: about 8 to 10 servings

WILD RICE DRESSING

- 1 cup minced onions
- 1 cup finely chopped celery
- ½ cup olive oil
- ½ cup chopped green pepper
- 2 green onions, finely chopped
- 1 tablespoon chopped fresh parsley
- 1 clove garlic, minced
- 1 teaspoon dried basil leaves
- 1 teaspoon ground black pepper
- ½ teaspoon ground sage
- ½ teaspoon dried rosemary leaves
- ½ teaspoon dried thyme leaves
- 1 package (6¼ ounces) long grain and wild rice, cooked according to package directions

Topped with crisp bacon and freshly grated cheese, creamy Parmesan Spinach and Artichokes will be a family favorite.

- 2 cups corn bread crumbs
- 1 can (14½ ounces) chicken broth
- 1 cup sliced fresh mushrooms

Preheat oven to 350 degrees. In a heavy large skillet over medium heat, cook minced onions and celery in olive oil until vegetables are almost tender. Add green pepper, green onions, parsley, and garlic to skillet; continue cooking 2 minutes, stirring frequently. Remove from heat; stir in basil, black pepper, sage, rosemary, and thyme until well blended. In a large bowl, combine onion mixture and remaining ingredients; spoon into a greased 8 x 11½-inch baking dish. Bake 35 to 40 minutes or until lightly browned. Serve warm.
Yield: about 8 to 10 servings

Delicate mushrooms are a tasty surprise in our Wild Rice Dressing (clockwise from left). *Orange zest and crystallized ginger awaken the flavor of Butternut Squash and Apple Purée, and Caramelized Onions have a buttery brown sugar glaze.*

CARAMELIZED ONIONS

- 2 pounds pearl onions, peeled
- 1/4 cup butter or margarine
- 2 tablespoons firmly packed brown sugar
- 1 tablespoon grated orange zest
- 1/8 teaspoon salt
- 1/8 teaspoon paprika

In a large saucepan, cover onions with water. Cover and cook over medium-high heat 10 to 12 minutes or until onions are almost tender; drain. In a heavy large skillet, combine onions and butter. Stirring frequently, cook over medium-high heat about 30 minutes or until golden brown. In a small bowl, combine remaining ingredients. Add brown sugar mixture to onions. Stirring constantly, cook until onions are evenly coated and browned. Serve warm.
Yield: about 6 servings

BUTTERNUT SQUASH AND APPLE PURÉE

- 1 butternut squash (about 2 1/2 pounds), peeled, seeded, and cut into 1/2-inch cubes
- 1 tart baking apple, peeled, cored, and coarsely chopped
- 2 tablespoons butter or margarine
- 1 tablespoon honey
- 1 teaspoon grated orange zest
- 1 teaspoon finely chopped crystallized ginger
- 1/8 teaspoon ground nutmeg

In a heavy large saucepan, cover squash and apple with water. Cover and cook over medium-high heat 15 to 20 minutes or until tender; drain. Reduce heat to medium-low; add remaining ingredients to squash mixture. Stirring constantly, cook squash mixture about 10 minutes or until smooth. Serve warm.
Yield: about 8 servings

Festive Herbed Zucchini Bundles are quick and easy to prepare in the microwave. Featuring a tangy poppy seed dressing, Spinach-Peach Salad (not shown) *is a fresh, colorful addition to the holiday table.*

HERBED ZUCCHINI BUNDLES

- 1 pound unpeeled zucchini, cut into 3-inch-long by 1/8-inch-thick julienne strips
- 2 medium sweet red peppers, sliced into ten 1/4-inch rings
- 2 tablespoons butter or margarine
- 1 teaspoon dried marjoram leaves
- 1/4 teaspoon dried oregano leaves

Divide zucchini strips into 10 equal bundles and place a pepper ring around each bundle. Place in a microwave-safe baking dish and cover with plastic wrap. Make 2 slits in top of plastic wrap. Microwave on medium-high power (90%) 3 1/2 to 4 minutes, turning dish halfway through cooking time. Remove dish from microwave. Place butter, marjoram, and oregano in a small microwave-safe bowl. Microwave on high power (100%) 20 to 30 seconds or until butter is melted; pour over zucchini. Serve warm.

Yield: 10 servings

SPINACH-PEACH SALAD

DRESSING
- 1/3 cup mayonnaise
- 1/4 cup orange juice
- 1 teaspoon sugar
- 1 teaspoon poppy seeds

SALAD
- 6 cups (about 10 ounces) fresh spinach, torn into bite-size pieces
- 1 can (29 ounces) peach slices, drained
- 1 medium red onion, sliced

For dressing, combine all ingredients until well blended.

For salad, toss together spinach, peaches, and onion in a large bowl. Cover and refrigerate salad and dressing in separate containers until ready to serve.

To serve, pour dressing over salad; toss until well coated.

Yield: about 12 servings

DEEP-DISH BERRY PIE

CRUST
- 2 1/4 cups all-purpose flour
- 1/2 teaspoon salt
- 1/2 cup chilled vegetable shortening
- 1/4 cup chilled butter or margarine
- 1/4 cup ice water

FILLING
- 2 cans (16 ounces each) tart red pitted cherries, drained
- 1 package (12 ounces) frozen whole blueberries
- 1 package (12 ounces) frozen whole red raspberries
- 1 1/2 cups plus 2 tablespoons sugar, divided
- 2 tablespoons fresh lemon juice
- 1/4 teaspoon ground cinnamon
- 1/3 cup cornstarch
- 1/3 cup cold water
- 2 tablespoons chilled butter or margarine
- 1 egg white, beaten

For crust, combine flour and salt in a medium bowl. Using a pastry blender or 2 knives, cut in shortening and butter until mixture resembles coarse meal. Sprinkle with water; mix until a soft dough forms. Shape dough into 2 balls. Wrap each ball with plastic wrap and chill while preparing filling.

For filling, combine cherries, blueberries, raspberries, 1 1/2 cups sugar, lemon juice, and cinnamon in a large saucepan over medium-high heat; stir until well blended. In a small bowl, combine cornstarch and water. Stirring constantly as fruit mixture begins to boil, add cornstarch mixture. Stir until mixture thickens. Remove from heat; place pan in cool water in sink. Allow filling to cool while rolling out dough.

Use a rolling pin to roll out half of dough between pieces of plastic wrap to 1/8-inch thickness. Transfer to a 9-inch deep-dish pie plate. Leaving 1/2-inch of dough over edge, use a sharp knife to trim dough. Cover crust and chill in refrigerator while filling cools to room temperature.

Preheat oven to 375 degrees. Roll out remaining dough for top crust. Spoon filling into bottom pie crust. Cut butter into small pieces and place over filling. Place top crust over filling; crimp edges of crust and make several slits in top. Brush with egg white and sprinkle remaining 2 tablespoons sugar over crust. Bake on a baking sheet 50 to 60 minutes or until crust is golden brown. (If edge of crust browns too quickly, cover edge with aluminum foil.) Serve warm.

Yield: about 10 servings

Remind guests to save room for Deep-Dish Berry Pie. The old-fashioned treat has a treasure of cherries, blueberries, and raspberries hidden beneath a flaky sugar-coated crust.

A luscious after-dinner delicacy, Pumpkin Cheesecake with Ginger Cream Topping has an irresistible whipped topping spiked with dark rum.

PUMPKIN CHEESECAKE WITH GINGER CREAM TOPPING

CRUST
- ³/₄ cup graham cracker crumbs
- ¹/₂ cup finely chopped pecans
- ¹/₄ cup firmly packed brown sugar
- ¹/₄ cup granulated sugar
- ¹/₄ cup butter or margarine, melted

FILLING
- 1 can (15 ounces) pumpkin
- 3 eggs
- ¹/₂ cup firmly packed brown sugar
- 1 teaspoon vanilla extract
- 1¹/₂ teaspoons ground cinnamon
- ¹/₂ teaspoon ground ginger
- ¹/₂ teaspoon ground nutmeg
- ¹/₄ teaspoon salt
- 3 packages (8 ounces each) cream cheese, softened
- ¹/₂ cup granulated sugar
- 1 tablespoon all-purpose flour

TOPPING
- 1 cup whipping cream
- 1 cup sour cream
- 2 tablespoons sugar
- 3 tablespoons dark rum
- ¹/₂ teaspoon vanilla extract
- ¹/₄ cup minced crystallized ginger
- 16 pecan halves to garnish

For crust, combine cracker crumbs, pecans, and sugars in a medium bowl until well blended; stir in melted butter. Press mixture into bottom and halfway up sides of a greased 9-inch springform pan; chill 1 hour.

Preheat oven to 350 degrees. For filling, beat pumpkin, eggs, brown sugar, vanilla, spices, and salt in a medium bowl. In a large bowl, beat cream cheese and granulated sugar until well blended. Beat flour and pumpkin mixture into cream cheese mixture until smooth. Pour filling into crust; bake 50 to 55 minutes or until center is set. Cool completely in pan.

For topping, chill a medium bowl and beaters from an electric mixer in freezer. In chilled bowl, beat whipping cream, sour cream, and sugar until stiff peaks form. Fold in rum, vanilla, and ginger. Spread topping over cheesecake. Cover and refrigerate overnight.

To serve, remove sides of pan and garnish top with pecan halves.
Yield: 16 servings

MOCHA-CARROT CAKE

CAKE

- 2 cups sugar
- ³/₄ cup vegetable oil
- ¹/₂ cup coffee-flavored liqueur
- 4 eggs
- 3 cups sifted all-purpose flour
- 1 tablespoon baking powder
- 1¹/₂ teaspoons ground cinnamon
- ¹/₂ teaspoon salt
- 3 cups shredded carrots
- 1 cup chopped walnuts
- ¹/₂ cup raisins

FROSTING

- 6 cups sifted confectioners sugar
- 2 packages (8 ounces each) cream cheese, softened
- 1 cup butter or margarine, softened
- 1 cup finely chopped walnuts

Preheat oven to 350 degrees. For cake, combine sugar, oil, liqueur, and eggs in a large bowl. Using high speed of an electric mixer, beat 3 minutes. Sift flour, baking powder, cinnamon, and salt into a medium bowl. Add dry ingredients to sugar mixture; beat until well blended. Stir in carrots, walnuts, and raisins. Pour batter into 2 greased and floured 9-inch round cake pans. Bake 30 to 35 minutes or until a toothpick inserted in center of cake comes out clean. Cool in pans 10 minutes. Remove from pans and cool completely on a wire rack.

For frosting, combine confectioners sugar, cream cheese, and butter in a large bowl; beat until smooth. Reserving 1¹/₂ cups frosting, spread remaining frosting between layers and on sides and top of cake.

To decorate cake, sprinkle walnuts on top of cake. Spoon reserved frosting into a pastry bag fitted with a small star tip. Pipe stripes of frosting 1 inch apart on top of cake in a lattice design. Pipe a decorative border around top and bottom edges of cake. Store in an airtight container in refrigerator.
Yield: about 16 servings

Coffee-flavored liqueur, walnuts, and raisins add richness to delicious Mocha-Carrot Cake.

HOME FOR THE HOLIDAYS

MENU

Orange-Carrot Soup

Dill Crackers

Stuffed Holiday Ham

Cheesy Spinach Soufflé

Creamy Garlic Mashed Potatoes

Pickled Yellow Squash

Cornmeal Yeast Muffins

Overnight Fruit Salad

Eggnog Custard Pie

Coconut-Orange Cake

Banana-Nut Cream Tart

A savory side dish, Cheesy Spinach Soufflé (clockwise from left) is loaded with Parmesan cheese. Inspired by two old-fashioned favorites — yeast rolls and corn bread — Cornmeal Yeast Muffins (recipe on page 70) offer whole kernels of golden corn in every bite. It's easy to make crunchy Pickled Yellow Squash (recipe on page 70) just like grandmother's! Cream cheese and butter make Creamy Garlic Mashed Potatoes extra smooth.

Dressed in a colorful medley of chopped greens, cabbage, and sweet red pepper, Stuffed Holiday Ham (recipe on page 70) *is cooked to succulent perfection.*

CHEESY SPINACH SOUFFLÉ

  1 container (16 ounces) cottage
     cheese
1 1/2 cups (about 6 ounces)
     shredded Parmesan cheese
  2 packages (10 ounces each)
     frozen chopped spinach,
     cooked and well drained
  2 eggs, separated
 1/4 cup butter or margarine, melted
  2 tablespoons minced onion
  1 clove garlic, minced
  2 tablespoons all-purpose flour
 1/2 teaspoon baking powder
 1/2 teaspoon lemon pepper

Preheat oven to 350 degrees. In a medium bowl, combine cottage cheese, Parmesan cheese, spinach, egg yolks, melted butter, onion, and garlic. In a small bowl, combine flour, baking powder, and lemon pepper. Add dry ingredients to spinach mixture; stir until well blended. In a small bowl, beat egg whites until stiff; fold into spinach mixture. Pour into a greased 2-quart soufflé dish. Bake uncovered 50 to 60 minutes or until center is set. Serve warm.
Yield: about 10 servings

CREAMY GARLIC MASHED POTATOES

  4 pounds russet potatoes, peeled
     and cut into pieces
  6 cloves garlic
  2 teaspoons salt, divided
  2 packages (3 ounces each)
     cream cheese, softened
 1/2 cup butter or margarine
  1 cup warm milk

Place potatoes in a Dutch oven. Cover with water; add garlic and 1 teaspoon salt. Cover and bring to a boil over medium-high heat. Reduce heat to medium and continue cooking 10 minutes or until potatoes are just tender; drain. Return potatoes and garlic to low heat. Add cream cheese, butter, and remaining 1 teaspoon salt; mash until cream cheese and butter are melted. Add milk and continue mashing until potatoes are coarsely mashed. Serve warm.
Yield: about 14 servings

CORNMEAL YEAST MUFFINS
(Shown on page 68)

	1	package dry yeast
	1/4	cup plus 1 teaspoon sugar,
			divided
	1/3	cup warm water (105 to
			115 degrees)
	1	cup milk
	1/2	cup butter or margarine
	1 1/2	teaspoons salt
	1	can (15 1/4 ounces) whole
			kernel corn, drained
	1	cup cream-style corn
	2	eggs, beaten
	1 1/2	cups yellow cornmeal
	3	cups all-purpose flour

In a small bowl, dissolve yeast and 1 teaspoon sugar in warm water. In a small saucepan, combine milk, butter, remaining 1/4 cup sugar, and salt over medium heat; whisk until butter melts and sugar is dissolved. Remove from heat and pour into a large bowl. Add whole kernel corn, cream-style corn, eggs, and yeast mixture; stir until well blended. Add cornmeal and flour, 1 cup at a time; stir until a thick batter forms. Cover and let rise in a warm place (80 to 85 degrees) 1 to 1 1/2 hours or until almost doubled in size.

Stir batter down. Spoon batter into greased muffin cups, filling each two-thirds full. Let rise uncovered in a warm place about 45 minutes.

Preheat oven to 375 degrees. Bake 20 to 25 minutes or until golden brown. Allow muffins to cool in pan 5 minutes. Serve warm or transfer to a wire rack to cool completely.
Yield: about 2 dozen muffins

PICKLED YELLOW SQUASH
(Shown on page 68)

	2	quarts cold water
	1	cup canning and pickling salt
	8	cups sliced yellow squash
	4	green peppers, chopped
	2	cups chopped white onions
	3	cups sugar
	2	cups white vinegar (5% acidity)

Lightly toasted Dill Crackers are great sprinkled atop tasty Orange-Carrot Soup. Served hot, the flavorful combo will chase away winter chills.

	1	teaspoon celery seed
	1	teaspoon mustard seed

In a large nonmetal bowl, combine water and salt; stir until well blended. Place squash in salt mixture. Cover and allow to stand 2 hours. Using a colander, drain and thoroughly rinse squash with cold water. In a large bowl, combine squash, peppers, and onions. Combine sugar, vinegar, celery seed, and mustard seed in a large Dutch oven (preferably enamelware). Bring vinegar mixture to a boil over high heat. Add vegetables; bring to a boil again. Spoon mixture into heat-resistant jars with lids; cool. Store in refrigerator.
Yield: about 5 pints pickled squash

STUFFED HOLIDAY HAM
(Shown on page 69)

	1	small head green cabbage,
			coarsely chopped
	1/2	pound mustard greens, spinach,
			or other fresh greens
	1	medium onion, quartered
	1	rib celery, coarsely chopped
	1	small sweet red pepper,
			quartered
	2	cloves garlic
	2	teaspoons crushed red pepper
			flakes
	8	to 9 pound fully cooked butt
			portion bone-in ham

Combine first 7 ingredients in small batches in a food processor; pulse process until finely chopped. Place ham in center of 2 layers of

cheesecloth large enough to cover ham. Make random cuts in ham down to the bone. Open cuts with fingers and stuff as much vegetable mixture as possible into each cut. Press remaining vegetable mixture onto surface of ham. Gather cheesecloth around ham; tie with kitchen string. Place stuffed ham in a large stockpot or roasting pan; add water to cover at least half of ham. Cover and bring water to a boil over high heat. Reduce heat to medium-low and simmer 1 1/2 to 2 hours or until vegetables are tender and ham is heated through, adding hot water as needed. Remove from heat and cool 1 hour. Remove ham from stockpot. Carefully unwrap cheesecloth, leaving vegetables on ham. Cover ham and refrigerate overnight. Serve chilled.
Yield: about 22 servings

ORANGE-CARROT SOUP

- 1/4 cup finely chopped onion
- 1 tablespoon butter or margarine
- 4 cups chicken or vegetable stock
- 1 pound carrots, shredded
- 1 can (11 ounces) mandarin oranges in syrup
- 1/2 cup orange juice
- 2 teaspoons grated orange zest
- 2 teaspoons honey
- 1/4 teaspoon ground ginger
- 1/4 cup cold water
- 1 tablespoon cornstarch
- 1/2 cup half and half

In a Dutch oven over medium heat, cook onion and butter about 5 minutes or until onion is clear. Add chicken stock and carrots. Increase heat to medium-high and bring to a boil. Reduce heat to medium; cook about 15 minutes or until carrots are almost tender. Remove from heat.

Remove 1 cup carrots from liquid using a slotted spoon; set aside. Add oranges and syrup, orange juice, orange zest, honey, and ginger to soup. Batch process soup in a food processor until puréed. Return soup to Dutch oven over medium heat. Add reserved carrots to soup; bring to a simmer. Combine cold water and

Sweet, tangy Overnight Fruit Salad combines pineapple chunks, cherries, mandarin orange slices, and miniature marshmallows in a creamy dressing.

cornstarch in a small bowl. Add cornstarch mixture and half and half to soup; stir until thickened. Serve warm with Dill Crackers.
Yield: about 8 cups soup

DILL CRACKERS

- 1 package (10 ounces) oyster crackers
- 1/4 cup vegetable oil
- 2 teaspoons dried dill weed

Preheat oven to 300 degrees. Place crackers in a large bowl. Combine oil and dill weed in a small bowl. Pour oil mixture over crackers; stir until well coated. Transfer to an ungreased jellyroll pan. Bake 15 minutes, stirring every 5 minutes. Place pan on a wire rack to cool. Store in an airtight container.
Yield: about 6 cups crackers

OVERNIGHT FRUIT SALAD

- 1 can (20 ounces) pineapple chunks in heavy syrup
- 3 egg yolks, beaten
- 2 tablespoons sugar

- 2 tablespoons white vinegar
- 1 tablespoon butter or margarine
- 1/8 teaspoon salt
- 2 cans (17 ounces each) pitted white Royal Anne cherries, drained
- 2 cans (11 ounces each) mandarin oranges, drained
- 1 1/2 cups miniature marshmallows
- 1 cup whipping cream, whipped

Drain pineapple, reserving 2 tablespoons syrup. In the top of a double boiler over hot water, combine egg yolks, sugar, vinegar, reserved pineapple syrup, butter, and salt. Stirring constantly, cook mixture about 4 minutes or until thickened. Transfer to a large bowl and let cool. Cover and chill 30 minutes.

Stir in pineapple, cherries, mandarin oranges, and marshmallows. Fold whipped cream into fruit mixture. Cover and chill overnight.
Yield: about 16 servings

Coconut-Orange Cake (left) *is a dreamy dessert featuring an orange-flavored filling between two layers of moist goodness. Iced with fluffy frosting accented with orange juice, the cake is covered with coconut. A new twist on a traditional treat, Eggnog Custard Pie is laced with bourbon and ground nutmeg.*

EGGNOG CUSTARD PIE

CRUST
- 1 1/2 cups all-purpose flour
- 1/4 teaspoon salt
- 1/2 cup vegetable shortening
- 1/4 cup water

FILLING
- 4 eggs
- 1/2 cup sugar
- 2 cups half and half
- 2 tablespoons bourbon
- 1 teaspoon vanilla extract
- 1/4 teaspoon ground nutmeg
- 1/8 teaspoon salt

TOPPING
- 1/2 cup whipping cream
- 1 1/2 tablespoons sugar
- 1 teaspoon bourbon

For crust, combine flour and salt in a medium bowl. Using a pastry blender or 2 knives, cut in shortening until mixture resembles coarse meal.

Sprinkle with water; mix until a soft dough forms. On a lightly floured surface, use a floured rolling pin to roll out dough to 1/8-inch thickness. Transfer to a 9-inch pie plate. Crimp edges of crust; use a sharp knife to trim excess crust.

Preheat oven to 450 degrees. For filling, beat eggs and sugar in a medium bowl until well blended. Add half and half; beat until smooth. Stir in bourbon, vanilla, nutmeg, and salt. Pour filling into crust. Bake 10 minutes. Reduce heat to 325 degrees and bake an additional 35 to 40 minutes or until a knife inserted in center of pie comes out clean. Cool pie on a wire rack.

For topping, beat whipping cream and sugar in a small bowl until stiff peaks form. Beat in bourbon. To serve, spoon topping onto each piece of pie.
Yield: about 8 servings

COCONUT-ORANGE CAKE

CAKE
- 1 package (18 1/4 ounces) yellow cake mix
- 3 eggs
- 1/3 cup vegetable oil
- 1 can (8 1/2 ounces) cream of coconut
- 1 cup sour cream

ORANGE FILLING
- 1/2 cup sugar
- 1 1/2 tablespoons all-purpose flour
- 1 can (11 ounces) mandarin oranges, drained
- 2 egg yolks (reserve egg whites for icing)
- 1/2 teaspoon butter or margarine
- 1/2 teaspoon vanilla extract

ICING
- 1 1/2 cups sugar
- 1/4 cup orange juice
- 2 egg whites
- 1 tablespoon light corn syrup

1/4 teaspoon cream of tartar
1 teaspoon vanilla extract
1 cup flaked coconut
  Mandarin orange segments to
    decorate

Preheat oven to 350 degrees. For cake, line bottoms of two 9-inch round cake pans with waxed paper. Grease paper and sides of pans. In a large bowl, combine cake mix, eggs, and oil; beat until well blended. Add cream of coconut and sour cream; beat until smooth. Pour batter into prepared pans. Bake 32 to 36 minutes or until a toothpick inserted in center of cake comes out clean. Cool in pans 10 minutes on a wire rack. Run knife around edge of pans to loosen cake; remove from pans and place on wire rack to cool completely.

For orange filling, combine sugar and flour in a heavy small saucepan. Add oranges, egg yolks, and butter. Stirring constantly, bring to a boil over medium heat; cook 4 minutes or until mixture thickens. Stir in vanilla. Cool to room temperature. Spread filling between cake layers.

For icing, combine sugar, orange juice, egg whites, corn syrup, and cream of tartar in top of a double boiler. Beat with a mixer until sugar is well blended. Place over boiling water and continue beating about 7 minutes or until soft peaks form. Remove from heat and add vanilla. Continue beating 2 minutes or until icing is desired consistency. Ice cake. Sprinkle coconut on top and sides of cake. Decorate with orange segments. Store in an airtight container in refrigerator.
Yield: about 16 servings

BANANA-NUT CREAM TART

FILLING
1/2 cup sugar
3 tablespoons all-purpose flour
3 cups half and half
3 eggs, beaten
3 tablespoons butter or margarine
3/4 teaspoon vanilla extract
1/4 teaspoon butter flavoring

Our Banana-Nut Cream Tart alternates banana slices and a light pudding on a crust of vanilla wafer crumbs and chopped pecans. Rows of bananas and caramelized nuts crown the yummy delight.

CRUST
1 cup vanilla wafer crumbs (about 20 cookies)
1 cup chopped pecans, toasted and coarsely ground
1/4 cup butter or margarine, softened
1/4 cup sugar

TOPPING
1 egg white
2 teaspoons water
1 cup chopped pecans
1/4 cup firmly packed brown sugar
2 tablespoons apple jelly
6 medium bananas

For filling, combine sugar and flour in the top of a double boiler. Add half and half, eggs, and butter; place over simmering water. Stirring frequently, cook about 20 minutes or until thick enough to coat back of a spoon. Stir in vanilla and butter flavoring. Remove from heat and pour into a medium bowl. Place plastic wrap directly on surface of filling; chill.

Preheat oven to 350 degrees. For

crust, combine all ingredients in a medium bowl. Press mixture into bottom and up sides of a lightly greased 8 x 11-inch tart pan with a removable bottom. Bake 10 to 12 minutes or until crust is firm; chill.

Reduce oven temperature to 225 degrees. For topping, combine egg white and water in a small bowl; beat until foamy. Stir in pecans and brown sugar. Spread coated pecans on an ungreased baking sheet. Bake 45 minutes, stirring every 15 minutes, or until golden brown. Cool pan on a wire rack.

To serve, melt apple jelly in a small saucepan over medium heat. Slice 2 bananas and place a single layer in pie crust. Spoon half of chilled filling over bananas. Place another single layer of 2 sliced bananas on filling. Top with remainder of filling. Alternate rows of caramelized nuts and slices of remaining bananas on top of filling. Brush melted apple jelly over bananas.
Yield: about 12 servings

CHRISTMAS FIESTA

MENU

Raspberry Lemonade

Jícama and Orange Salad with Lime Dressing

Chicken and Rice Soup

Flour Tortillas

Pork Tamales with Red Pepper and Green Chile Cream Sauces

Posole Casserole

Pecan Pralines

Candied Pumpkin

Mexican Sugar Cookies

PORK TAMALES WITH RED PEPPER AND GREEN CHILE CREAM SAUCES

Prepare meat mixture a day ahead for easy assembly of tamales.

- 7 pound pork shoulder roast, boned, saving bone
- 2 heads garlic, separated into cloves
- 9 cups water
- 1/3 cup plus 1/4 cup chili powder, divided
- 4 teaspoons cumin seed
- 3 teaspoons salt, divided
- 1 package (8 ounces) dried corn shucks
- 1 package (4.4 pounds) masa harina (about 16 cups)
- 2 pounds (4 cups) shortening or lard
- 1 can (14.5 ounces) beef broth

Cut pork into 3-inch pieces. Place meat, bone, and garlic in a stockpot. Add 9 cups water, and more if necessary, to cover meat; bring to a boil over medium-high heat. Reduce heat to medium-low; cover and simmer about 2 hours or until meat is tender. Place meat and liquid in separate containers; discard bone. Shred meat by hand or in a food processor. Place meat in a heavy Dutch oven and stir in 1/3 cup chili powder, cumin seed, and 1 teaspoon salt. Add about 3 cups of reserved liquid to Dutch oven. Stirring frequently, cover and simmer over low heat 1 hour to allow flavors to blend. If necessary, add additional liquid to prevent meat from sticking to pan. Cover and chill meat and reserved liquid overnight in separate containers.

Steamed in corn shucks to seal in the flavor, savory Pork Tamales offer a shredded-meat filling in a traditional masa harina dough. To accompany the entrée, there are two wonderful toppings, Red Pepper and Green Chile Cream Sauces.

Place corn shucks in warm water about 30 minutes to soften. Clean and separate corn shucks.

For tamale dough, combine masa harina, remaining 1/4 cup chili powder, and remaining 2 teaspoons salt in a large bowl. Cut shortening into masa mixture until it resembles coarse meal. Skim fat from chilled liquid. If necessary, add beef broth to reserved liquid to make 8 cups. Gradually add liquid to mixture, stirring until a soft dough forms that will stick together.

To assemble each tamale, place a softened corn shuck on a flat surface with a long side facing you. Spread about 1/4 cup dough from wide end about 4 1/2 inches along one side. Continue to spread dough, forming a rectangle that covers about two-thirds of the wide end of corn shuck (**Fig. 1**).

Fig. 1

Spread a heaping tablespoon of meat down center of dough (**Fig. 2**).

Fig. 2

Roll edge closest to you over meat, rolling back corn shuck enough to expose a small amount of dough (**Fig. 3**).

Fig. 3

Bring far side toward you until dough edges overlap; wrap corn shuck around tamale. Fold narrow end of corn shuck over tamale. Stand individual tamales in a container or tie in bundles with kitchen string and stand with open ends up (**Fig. 4**).

Fig. 4

(**Note:** Tamales may be chilled or frozen at this point and steamed at a later time.)

To steam tamales, stand tamales with open ends up in a steamer basket placed over hot water in a stockpot. Cover and steam 1 to 1 1/2 hours. Serve warm with Red Pepper Cream Sauce and Green Chile Cream Sauce.

Yield: about 5 1/2 dozen tamales

RED PEPPER CREAM SAUCE
- 1/4 cup butter or margarine
- 1 large sweet red pepper, chopped
- 1/4 cup thinly sliced green onions
- 3 tablespoons all-purpose flour
- 1/2 teaspoon salt
- 1/4 teaspoon ground white pepper
- 1 1/2 cups half and half
- 1 tablespoon freshly squeezed lemon juice
  Sweet red pepper strips to garnish

Continued on page 76

In a medium saucepan, melt butter over medium heat. Add red pepper and onions; cook until almost tender. Reserve 2 tablespoons pepper mixture. Place remaining pepper mixture in a food processor and purée. Return mixture to saucepan and reduce heat to medium-low. Stirring constantly, add flour, salt, and white pepper to mixture. Cook 2 minutes or until flour is well blended and sauce thickens. While whisking mixture, gradually add half and half and lemon juice. Stir in reserved pepper mixture. Increase heat to medium; continue cooking 5 minutes or until mixture thickens. Garnish with sweet red pepper strips. Serve warm over Pork Tamales.
Yield: about 2¹/₂ cups sauce

GREEN CHILE CREAM SAUCE

- ¹/₄ cup butter or margarine
- ¹/₄ cup thinly sliced green onions
- 3 cans (4¹/₂ ounces each) chopped green chiles
- 2 tablespoons seeded and finely chopped fresh jalapeño peppers
- 2 tablespoons all-purpose flour
- ¹/₄ teaspoon salt
- ¹/₄ teaspoon ground white pepper
- 1¹/₂ cups half and half
- 2 teaspoons freshly squeezed lime juice

In a medium saucepan, melt butter over medium heat. Add onions; cook until almost tender. Add undrained green chiles and jalapeño peppers; stirring frequently, cook 2 minutes. Reduce heat to medium-low; stirring constantly, add flour, salt, and white pepper to mixture. Cook 1 minute or until flour is well blended and sauce thickens. While whisking mixture, gradually add half and half and lime juice; continue cooking 5 minutes or until mixture thickens. Serve warm over Pork Tamales.
Yield: about 3¹/₄ cups sauce

JÍCAMA AND ORANGE SALAD WITH LIME DRESSING

LIME DRESSING

- ¹/₂ cup sugar
- 1 tablespoon dry mustard
- ³/₄ cup peanut oil
- 6 tablespoons freshly squeezed lime juice
- ¹/₄ cup honey
- 3 tablespoons water
- ¹/₄ cup white wine vinegar
- 2 tablespoons chopped fresh cilantro

SALAD

Leaf lettuce
- 4 to 5 cups peeled, matchsticked jícama
- 5 navel oranges, peeled and sectioned
Seeds of 2 pomegranates
Finely chopped, unsalted, dry-roasted peanuts

For lime dressing, combine sugar and dry mustard in a medium bowl. Add oil, lime juice, honey, water, and vinegar; stir until well blended. Stir in cilantro.

For salad, layer ingredients in order given. Serve with lime dressing.
Yield: about 14 servings

FLOUR TORTILLAS
(Shown on page 78)

- 2 cups all-purpose flour
- ³/₄ teaspoon baking powder
- ¹/₂ teaspoon salt
- ¹/₄ cup vegetable shortening or lard
- 8 tablespoons water

In a medium bowl, combine flour, baking powder, and salt. Using a pastry blender or 2 knives, cut in shortening until mixture resembles coarse meal. Add water, stirring until well blended.

Turn dough onto a lightly floured surface. Gradually sprinkle dough with additional water as necessary to shape into a ball. Knead dough 3 to

5 minutes or until smooth and elastic. Divide dough into 12 balls. Cover with plastic wrap and let rest at room temperature 30 minutes.

Heat an ungreased griddle or large skillet over medium-high heat. Working with 1 ball of dough at a time on a very lightly floured surface, roll into a 7-inch circle. To form a circle, rotate dough and turn over every few strokes of the rolling pin. On hot griddle, cook tortilla about 1 minute on each side or until lightly browned. Transfer tortilla onto a platter and cover with a lid or wrap in a kitchen towel and aluminum foil to retain moisture. Repeat with remaining dough. Wrapped tortillas may be placed in a 200-degree oven for a short period of time to remain warm. To reheat, place foil-wrapped tortillas in a 325-degree oven 15 to 20 minutes.
Yield: twelve 7-inch tortillas

RASPBERRY LEMONADE

- 3 cups sugar
- 1 cup water
- 1 package (12 ounces) frozen whole red raspberries, thawed, **or** 1 cup raspberry juice
- 1¹/₂ cups freshly squeezed lemon juice (about 10 to 12 small lemons)
- 1 tablespoon grated lemon zest
- 5 to 6 cups club soda, chilled Lemon slices to garnish

In a medium saucepan, combine sugar and water over medium heat; stir until sugar dissolves. Increase heat to medium-high and bring to a boil. Stirring constantly, boil 1 minute. Pour sugar syrup into a heat-resistant medium bowl and allow to cool.

Press raspberries through a sieve over another medium bowl. Discard seeds and pulp. Add lemon juice, raspberry juice, and lemon zest to sugar syrup; cover and chill.

To serve, combine juice mixture and club soda to taste. Garnish with lemon slices.
Yield: about thirteen 6-ounce servings

Garnished with lemon slices, tangy Raspberry Lemonade will have your guests asking for more. Jícama and Orange Salad with Lime Dressing is a crisp and colorful combination that includes sweet, tart pomegranate seeds and nutty slivers of Mexican jícama. It's great with our tamales!

Fresh, hand-rolled Flour Tortillas (recipe on page 76) are just right for dipping in our delicious Chicken and Rice Soup. Chopped green chiles and cumin give the soup a hot, peppery flavor.

CHICKEN AND RICE SOUP

3 pound broiler-fryer chicken
  (discard giblets)
6¹/₂ cups water
1 medium onion, cut into large
  pieces
2 ribs celery with leaves, cut into
  pieces
1 clove garlic
1 bay leaf
1 cup thinly sliced carrots
²/₃ cup uncooked long-grain rice
¹/₂ cup finely chopped onion
1 can (4¹/₂ ounces) chopped
  green chiles
2 chicken bouillon cubes

¹/₄ teaspoon salt
¹/₄ teaspoon ground white pepper
¹/₄ teaspoon ground cumin
  Chopped green onions to garnish

Place chicken, water, onion pieces, celery, garlic, and bay leaf in a stockpot over high heat; bring to a boil. Cover and reduce heat to medium-low; simmer 1 hour or until chicken is tender. Strain chicken stock and chill; discard vegetables. Skin and bone chicken. Cut meat into bite-size pieces; chill.

Skim fat from chicken stock. Combine chicken stock, carrots, rice, chopped onion, green chiles, bouillon, salt, white pepper, and cumin in a Dutch oven over medium-high heat; bring mixture to a boil. Reduce heat to low; cover and simmer 30 minutes, adding chicken pieces during last 10 minutes. Garnish with green onions and serve warm.
Yield: about 9 cups soup

Inspired by an authentic Mexican Christmas dish, Posole Casserole is a spicy concoction of zucchini, hominy, and onions stirred together with a generous portion of Monterey Jack and Cheddar cheeses.

POSOLE CASSEROLE

2   medium onions, coarsely
    chopped
3   tablespoons vegetable oil
1   medium zucchini, diced
4   cloves garlic, minced
1   tablespoon chili powder
2   teaspoons ground cumin
2   cans (15¹/₂ ounces each)
    yellow hominy, drained
1   tablespoon freshly squeezed
    lime juice
¹/₂   teaspoon salt
¹/₂   teaspoon ground black pepper

1   cup (4 ounces) combined
    shredded Monterey Jack and
    Cheddar cheese
¹/₄   cup fresh cilantro leaves,
    chopped
    Fresh cilantro leaves to garnish

Cook onions in oil in a heavy large skillet over medium-high heat 5 minutes or until onions begin to soften. Stirring frequently, add zucchini, garlic, chili powder, and cumin; cook about 5 minutes or until onions begin to brown.

Reduce heat to medium-low. Add hominy, lime juice, salt, and pepper; stir until well blended. Continue cooking until hominy is heated through. Remove from heat. Stir in cheese and chopped cilantro. Garnish with cilantro leaves and serve warm.
Yield: about 12 servings

PECAN PRALINES

2 cups sugar
1 teaspoon baking soda
1 cup buttermilk
1 tablespoon light corn syrup
3/4 cup butter, cut into small pieces
2 cups chopped pecans
1 teaspoon vanilla extract

Butter sides of a heavy Dutch oven. Combine sugar and baking soda in buttered pan. Add buttermilk and corn syrup. Stirring constantly, cook over medium-low heat until sugar dissolves. Using a pastry brush dipped in hot water, wash down any sugar crystals on sides of pan. Attach a candy thermometer to pan, making sure thermometer does not touch bottom of pan. Increase heat to medium and bring to a boil. Cook, stirring constantly, until syrup reaches 210 degrees on thermometer; add butter. Continue stirring and cooking mixture until syrup reaches soft-ball stage (approximately 234 to 240 degrees). Test about 1/2 teaspoon syrup in ice water. Syrup will easily form a ball in ice water but will flatten when held in your hand. Place pan in 2 inches of cold water in sink. Cool to approximately 140 degrees. Using medium speed of an electric mixer, beat candy until thickened and no longer glossy. Quickly stir in pecans and vanilla. Drop by tablespoonfuls onto lightly greased waxed paper. Allow pralines to cool completely. Wrap pralines individually in cellophane or plastic wrap and store in an airtight container.
Yield: about 2 1/2 dozen pralines

CANDIED PUMPKIN

8 cups 1-inch cubes of fresh pumpkin (about a 5-pound pumpkin)
1/2 cup firmly packed brown sugar
1/4 cup granulated sugar
1 1/2 tablespoons all-purpose flour
1/2 teaspoon ground cinnamon
1/2 teaspoon salt
1/4 teaspoon ground allspice
3/4 cup orange juice
1/4 cup maple syrup
3 tablespoons butter or margarine, softened
Chopped toasted pecans to serve

Preheat oven to 350 degrees. Place pumpkin pieces in a single layer on a lightly greased 10 1/2 x 15 1/2 x 1-inch jellyroll pan; set aside. In a medium saucepan, combine sugars, flour, cinnamon, salt, and allspice. Add orange juice, maple syrup, and butter, stirring until well blended. Stirring occasionally, cook over medium heat about 5 minutes. Pour over pumpkin. Spooning syrup over pumpkin every 15 minutes, bake 1 hour or until pumpkin is hot and syrup is bubbly. Transfer to serving dishes; sprinkle with pecans. Serve warm.
Yield: about 12 servings

MEXICAN SUGAR COOKIES

3/4 cup vegetable oil
2 eggs
1 1/2 teaspoons vanilla extract
1 1/4 cups sugar, divided
2 cups all-purpose flour
1 teaspoon baking powder
1/4 teaspoon salt
1 1/2 teaspoons ground cinnamon

Preheat oven to 400 degrees. In a large bowl, beat oil, eggs, and vanilla until well blended. Add 1 cup sugar; beat until smooth. In a small bowl, combine flour, baking powder, and salt. Add flour mixture to oil mixture; stir until a soft dough forms. In a small bowl, combine remaining 1/4 cup sugar and cinnamon. Drop teaspoonfuls of dough into cinnamon-sugar mixture; roll into balls. Place balls 2 inches apart on a greased baking sheet. Flatten cookies with bottom of a glass dipped in cinnamon-sugar mixture. Bake 4 to 6 minutes or until bottoms are lightly browned. Transfer cookies to a wire rack to cool. Store in a cookie tin.
Yield: about 4 1/2 dozen cookies

Pecan Pralines (bottom, on plate) *are irresistible caramelized candy patties packed with lots of crunchy nuts. Mexican Sugar Cookies offer an old-fashioned favorite flavored with cinnamon. Served hot and bubbly, Candied Pumpkin* (in dessert cup) *is sprinkled with toasted pecans.*

OLDE ENGLISH CHARM

MENU

Seafood Chowder

Rye Bread

Roast Goose

Sausage-Pecan Stuffing

Red Cabbage and Apples

Creamy Mint Carrots

Spinach-Herb Pie

Plum Pudding with Brandy Butter Sauce

Victorian Stamped Cookies

Golden Roast Goose, garnished with fresh parsley and fruit, makes a magnificent showing on your holiday table. Apples and apricots lend a hint of sweetness to savory Sausage-Pecan Stuffing (right).

ROAST GOOSE

    1   goose (about 10 pounds)
    2   tablespoons olive oil
    2   cups water
    2   cups apple cider, divided
 1/4   cup soy sauce
    2   tablespoons cornstarch
    2   tablespoons water
        Fresh orange slices, parsley,
           and cranberries to garnish

Remove giblets, neck, and fat from inside goose; discard fat. Preheat oven to 450 degrees. Rinse goose and pat dry. Lift wing tips up and over back so they are tucked under bird. Rub goose with oil and place breast side up in a large roasting pan. Insert meat thermometer into thickest part of thigh, making sure thermometer does not touch bone. Bake uncovered 40 to 45 minutes or until skin is crisp.

While goose is cooking, combine giblets, neck, and 2 cups water in a medium saucepan; bring to a boil, reduce heat, and simmer 30 minutes. Remove from heat and discard giblets and neck. Stir in 1 cup cider and soy sauce; set aside. Remove goose from oven; reduce oven temperature to 350 degrees. Pour cider mixture over goose. Cover with aluminum foil. Basting every 20 minutes with cider mixture, bake about 1 hour 30 minutes or until thermometer registers 180 degrees and juices run clear when thickest part of thigh is pierced with a fork. Reserve 1/2 cup meat drippings for sauce. Transfer goose to a serving platter and let stand 20 minutes before carving. Garnish goose with orange slices, parsley, and cranberries.

For sauce, combine cornstarch and water in a small bowl; stir until smooth. In a medium saucepan, combine reserved meat drippings and remaining 1 cup cider; bring to a boil. Stirring constantly, add cornstarch mixture to sauce and cook 5 to 7 minutes or until thickened and heated through. Serve warm sauce with goose.
Yield: about 8 servings

Old-fashioned Seafood Chowder is loaded with chunks of fish, scallops, onions, and potatoes. Molasses adds richness to dark, hearty Rye Bread (recipe on page 84).

SAUSAGE-PECAN STUFFING

    1   pound mild pork sausage
    1   onion, chopped
    1   cup coarsely chopped celery
    4   cups coarsely crumbled corn
           bread
    3   cups plain croutons
    3   apples, peeled, cored, and diced
    1   cup chopped pecans
 1/2   cup chopped dried apricots
    2   tablespoons ground sage
    2   teaspoons poultry seasoning
    1   teaspoon salt
 1/2   teaspoon ground black pepper
    4   eggs, beaten
    1   can (14 1/2 ounces) chicken broth

In a medium skillet, cook sausage until brown. Reserving drippings, transfer sausage to paper towels to drain; crumble sausage. Add onion and celery to drippings in skillet; cook until tender. Remove from heat. Preheat oven to 375 degrees. In a large bowl, combine next 9 ingredients. Stir in onion mixture, sausage, eggs, and chicken broth. Spoon into a greased 9 x 13-inch baking dish; cover and bake 50 minutes. Uncover and bake 10 minutes longer or until top is brown. Serve warm.
Yield: about 10 servings

SEAFOOD CHOWDER

    2   pounds orange roughy, halibut,
           or haddock fillets, cut into
           bite-size pieces
    1   pound bay scallops
    3   cups water
 1/4   pound salt pork, diced
    6   onions, chopped
    2   tablespoons all-purpose flour
    2   cups peeled, diced red potatoes
 2 1/2 cups milk
 1/2   cup dry white wine
 1/2   cup finely chopped fresh parsley
    2   tablespoons butter or margarine
    1   teaspoon salt
    1   teaspoon ground black pepper

In a large saucepan, combine fish, scallops, and water; bring to a boil over medium heat. Reduce heat and simmer 30 minutes. Reserving liquid, strain seafood.

In a stockpot, cook salt pork over medium high heat until golden brown. Reserving drippings, transfer salt pork to a medium bowl. Add onions to drippings in stockpot; cook until tender. Add onions to salt pork in bowl. Stir flour into drippings in stockpot and cook 1 minute. Stirring constantly,

Continued on page 84

gradually add reserved seafood liquid. Add potatoes, onion mixture, and seafood. Cover and simmer over medium-low heat 40 to 45 minutes. Stir in remaining ingredients. Cook until heated through (do not boil). Serve warm.
Yield: about 15 servings

RYE BREAD

(Shown on page 83)

2¹/₂ cups warm water
¹/₄ cup butter or margarine, melted
3 packages dry yeast
¹/₂ cup molasses
2 tablespoons caraway seed
1 tablespoon white vinegar
1 teaspoon salt
4 cups rye flour
4 cups bread flour
　Vegetable cooking spray

In a large bowl, combine water and butter. Add yeast; stir until dissolved. Stir in molasses, caraway seed, vinegar, and salt. Add flours and stir until a soft dough forms. Turn onto a lightly floured surface and knead 5 minutes or until dough becomes smooth and elastic. Place in a large bowl sprayed with cooking spray, turning once to coat top of dough. Cover and let rise in a warm place (80 to 85 degrees) 1 hour or until doubled in size. Turn dough onto a lightly floured surface and punch down. Divide dough into three equal pieces; shape each piece into a loaf. Place in separate 5 x 9-inch loaf pans sprayed with cooking spray; spray tops of dough. Cover and let rise in a warm place 1 hour or until doubled in size.
Preheat oven to 375 degrees. Bake 25 to 30 minutes or until bread sounds hollow when tapped. Serve warm.
Yield: 3 loaves bread

Served with a lightly sweetened sauce, Creamy Mint Carrots (left) offer a delightful flavor combination. The colorful Red Cabbage and Apples is simmered in a tangy broth.

RED CABBAGE AND APPLES

¹/₄ cup butter or margarine
2 onions, chopped
2 teaspoons salt
³/₄ teaspoon ground black pepper
¹/₂ teaspoon ground nutmeg
2 pounds red cabbage, chopped
4 apples, peeled, cored, and sliced
1 can (14¹/₂ ounces) chicken broth
3 tablespoons lemon juice
2 tablespoons apple cider vinegar

In a Dutch oven, melt butter over medium heat. Stir in onions, salt, pepper, and nutmeg; cook until onions are tender. Stir in cabbage, apples, chicken broth, lemon juice, and vinegar; bring to a boil. Reduce heat to medium-low, cover, and simmer 25 to 30 minutes or until cabbage and apples are tender. Serve warm.
Yield: about 12 servings

CREAMY MINT CARROTS

5 cups thinly sliced carrots (about 1¹/₂ pounds)
3 cups plus 2 teaspoons water, divided
1 teaspoon cornstarch
1 cup whipping cream
¹/₄ cup firmly packed brown sugar
¹/₄ cup chopped fresh mint leaves
2 tablespoons butter or margarine
1 teaspoon salt
¹/₂ teaspoon ground black pepper

Cover carrots with 3 cups water in a large saucepan; bring to a boil. Cook carrots 3 to 5 minutes or until just tender; drain carrots and return to pan.
In a small bowl, combine cornstarch and 2 teaspoons water; stir until smooth. In a small saucepan, bring cream to a boil. Whisking constantly, add cornstarch mixture to cream, bring to a boil, and cook until thickened. Stir in remaining ingredients. Stir cream mixture into carrots. Serve warm.
Yield: about 10 servings

SPINACH-HERB PIE

CRUST
1 1/2 cups all-purpose flour
1/2 teaspoon salt
1/2 cup vegetable shortening
3 to 4 tablespoons cold water

FILLING
1 cup half and half
1 cup milk
4 eggs
1 teaspoon ground nutmeg
1 teaspoon salt
1/2 teaspoon ground black pepper
1/2 cup butter or margarine
1 onion, chopped
1 teaspoon dried tarragon leaves, crushed
1 teaspoon dried basil leaves, crushed
1 teaspoon dried thyme leaves, crushed
1 tablespoon all-purpose flour
2 packages (10 ounces each) frozen chopped spinach, thawed and well drained
1 cup (4 ounces) shredded mozzarella cheese
1 egg, beaten
Green, red, and yellow liquid food coloring

For crust, combine flour and salt in a medium bowl. Using a pastry blender or 2 knives, cut in shortening until mixture resembles coarse meal. Sprinkle with water; mix until a soft dough forms. On a lightly floured surface, use a floured rolling pin to roll out dough to 1/8-inch thickness. Use a sharp knife to cut out a 9 x 13-inch rectangle and three 3 1/2-inch-long holly leaves. Use knife to make veins in leaves. Shape small pieces of dough scraps into 9 berries. Reserve remaining dough scraps. Cover all dough and set aside.

Preheat oven to 350 degrees. For filling, whisk first 6 ingredients in a medium bowl. In a large skillet, melt butter over medium heat. Add onion, tarragon, basil, and thyme; cook until onion is tender. Stir in flour; cook

Cheesy Spinach-Herb Pie is seasoned with tarragon, basil, and thyme and dressed up with a holly sprig made from pastry scraps.

1 minute. Stirring constantly, gradually add half and half mixture. Cook 3 to 5 minutes or until slightly thickened. Stir in spinach. Pour filling into a greased 7 x 11-inch baking dish. Sprinkle cheese over spinach mixture. Place crust over filling and use a sharp knife to trim edges. Brush with beaten egg. Arrange holly leaves on crust. Shape stems from reserved dough scraps and arrange on crust. Arrange berries on crust. Brush pastry decorations with beaten egg. Use a paintbrush and food coloring to paint leaves green, berries red, and stems brown (green, red, and yellow combined). Bake 50 to 55 minutes or until crust is golden brown. Serve warm.

Yield: about 10 servings

PLUM PUDDING WITH BRANDY BUTTER SAUCE

PLUM PUDDING
- 1 pound pitted prunes, chopped
- 1 cup brandy
- 2¹/₂ cups all-purpose flour
- 2 teaspoons baking powder
- 1 teaspoon salt
- ¹/₂ teaspoon baking soda
- ¹/₂ teaspoon ground cinnamon
- ¹/₂ teaspoon ground cloves
- ¹/₄ teaspoon ground nutmeg
- ¹/₄ teaspoon ground mace
- ¹/₂ cup butter or margarine, softened
- ¹/₂ cup granulated sugar
- 3 eggs
- 1 cup molasses
- ¹/₂ teaspoon dried grated lemon peel
- 1 cup buttermilk
- 1 cup chopped walnuts

SAUCE
- 2 cups sifted confectioners sugar
- 1 cup butter or margarine
- 1 cup whipping cream
- 2 tablespoons brandy
- 1 teaspoon vanilla extract
  Ground nutmeg to garnish

For plum pudding, combine prunes and brandy in a medium bowl. Cover and let stand at room temperature overnight.

Preheat oven to 325 degrees. Sift flour, baking powder, salt, baking soda, cinnamon, cloves, nutmeg, and mace into a medium bowl. In a large bowl, cream butter and sugar until fluffy. Add eggs, molasses, and lemon peel; beat until smooth. Beat dry ingredients and buttermilk alternately into creamed mixture. Stir in walnuts and prunes (including brandy). Pour batter into a greased and floured 9-inch springform pan. Bake 1 hour 30 minutes, cover with aluminum foil, and bake about 15 minutes longer or until a toothpick inserted in center comes out clean. Cool in pan 10 minutes; remove sides of pan.

For sauce, combine confectioners sugar, butter, and whipping cream in a medium saucepan. Stirring constantly, cook over medium heat until sugar dissolves and mixture comes to a boil. Stirring constantly, cook 3 minutes or until thickened. Remove from heat; stir in brandy and vanilla. Garnish with nutmeg. Cut pudding into wedges and serve with warm sauce.
Yield: about 18 servings

VICTORIAN STAMPED COOKIES

- ³/₄ cup butter or margarine, softened
- ³/₄ cup firmly packed brown sugar
- 1 egg
- 1 teaspoon vanilla extract
- ¹/₂ teaspoon butter extract
- 2¹/₄ cups all-purpose flour
- ¹/₈ teaspoon salt

In a large bowl, cream butter and brown sugar until fluffy. Add egg and extracts; beat until smooth. In a medium bowl, combine flour and salt. Add dry ingredients to creamed mixture; stir until a soft dough forms. Cover dough and chill 1 hour.

Preheat oven to 350 degrees. Shape dough into 1-inch balls and place 2 inches apart on a greased baking sheet. Flatten balls with 2-inch-diameter cookie stamps (prepared according to manufacturer's directions). Bake 9 to 11 minutes or until bottoms are lightly browned. Transfer cookies to a wire rack to cool. Store in an airtight container.
Yield: about 5 dozen cookies

Lightly embossed with cookie stamps, Victorian Stamped Cookies are pretty and palate-pleasing.

While the Christmas puddings of olden days often took weeks to prepare, our delectable Plum Pudding is a pleasingly modern variation. It's served with sweet Brandy Butter Sauce as a grand finale to your meal.

Tickle your guests' fancies with the bubbly flavor of Sparkling Wine Punch (recipe on page 89). *A fruited ice ring makes the beverage especially festive.*

BEEF SATÉ WITH HOT PEANUT DIPPING SAUCE

HOT PEANUT DIPPING SAUCE
- ¼ cup smooth peanut butter
- ¼ cup beef broth
- 2 tablespoons peanut oil
- 1 tablespoon soy sauce
- 1 tablespoon seasoned rice wine vinegar
- 1 teaspoon dark sesame oil
- 1 teaspoon freshly grated ginger
- ½ teaspoon crushed red pepper flakes

BEEF SATÉ
- ¾ cup seasoned rice wine vinegar
- ⅓ cup peanut oil
- ⅓ cup soy sauce

- 3 cloves garlic, minced
- 1 tablespoon firmly packed brown sugar
- 1 tablespoon grated fresh ginger
- 1 teaspoon crushed red pepper flakes
- 2 pounds flank steak, trimmed of fat and partially frozen
- Six-inch-long bamboo skewers

For hot peanut dipping sauce, combine all ingredients in a food processor; process until well blended. Transfer to a small bowl; cover and let stand at room temperature 2 hours to allow flavors to blend. Store in refrigerator.

For beef saté, combine vinegar, oil, soy sauce, garlic, brown sugar, ginger, and red pepper flakes in a large bowl; stir until well blended. Slice chilled meat diagonally across the grain into thin slices. Place beef strips in marinade and refrigerate overnight. Soak bamboo skewers in water overnight.

Bring sauce to room temperature. Thread marinated beef strips onto skewers. Broil or grill about 4 inches from heat 5 to 6 minutes; turning once after 3 minutes. Serve warm with sauce.

Yield: about ½ cup sauce and about 4 dozen appetizers

ROASTED GARLIC

- 6 large heads garlic
- 1 loaf (8 ounces) 2¹/₂-inch-diameter French bread, cut into ¹/₄-inch slices

Preheat oven to 375 degrees. Remove the outermost papery skin from each head of garlic, leaving cloves of garlic intact. Slice across stem end of each garlic head. Place garlic heads in a baking dish; cover with heavy aluminum foil. Bake about 1 hour. Allow garlic to cool 10 to 15 minutes before serving. Place French bread slices on a baking sheet. Toast in a 375-degree oven 5 minutes, turning slices over after 3 minutes. To serve, press garlic pulp out of each clove and spread on toast.
Yield: about 50 servings

CURRIED BLUE CHEESECAKE

- 1¹/₄ cups butter-flavored cracker crumbs
- ¹/₄ cup freshly grated Parmesan cheese
- ¹/₄ cup butter or margarine, melted
- 3 packages (8 ounces each) cream cheese, softened
- 4 eggs
- ¹/₂ cup mayonnaise
- ¹/₂ cup finely minced onion
- 1 tablespoon lemon juice
- ³/₄ teaspoon curry powder
- ¹/₂ teaspoon Worcestershire sauce
- 8 ounces blue cheese, crumbled
  Purchased chutney to garnish
  Crackers to serve

Preheat oven to 300 degrees. In a medium bowl, combine cracker crumbs, Parmesan cheese, and melted butter. Press into bottom of a greased 9-inch springform pan. In a large bowl, beat cream cheese until fluffy. Add eggs, 1 at a time, beating 2 minutes after each addition. Continue beating while adding mayonnaise, onion, lemon juice, curry powder, and Worcestershire sauce; beat until well blended. Stir in blue cheese. Pour filling

Garnished with chutney and served with crackers, Curried Blue Cheesecake (clockwise from top left) *is a robust appetizer. Simple Roasted Garlic is a buttery-soft spread for toasted slices of French bread. Marinated Beef Saté is terrific grilled or broiled. Our Hot Peanut Dipping Sauce is the perfect condiment for these tender skewered tidbits.*

over crust. Bake 1¹/₂ hours. Turn oven off. With oven door partially open, leave cheesecake in oven 1 hour. Transfer to a wire rack to cool. Remove sides of pan. Spoon chutney over top of cheesecake. Serve chilled or at room temperature with crackers.
Yield: about 50 servings

Warm up holiday guests with steaming Mushroom Soup, which is loaded with fresh sliced mushrooms in a well-seasoned beef broth. The homemade goodness of our Herbed Breadsticks will keep guests coming back for more.

MUSHROOM SOUP

　1　pound fresh mushrooms
　1/4　cup butter or margarine
　1　onion, coarsely chopped
　2　ribs celery, coarsely chopped
　2　cloves garlic, minced
　6　cups beef broth
　1　teaspoon dried thyme leaves
　1/2　teaspoon dried parsley flakes
　1　bay leaf
　　　Chopped fresh parsley to garnish

Separate mushroom caps from stems; set aside. Coarsely chop mushroom stems. In a Dutch oven over medium heat, combine mushroom stems, butter, onion, celery, and garlic; sauté about 8 minutes or until tender. Add beef broth, thyme, dried parsley, and bay leaf. Cover and reduce heat to medium-low; simmer about 45 minutes. Strain and return liquid to Dutch oven. Discard cooked vegetables. Slice mushroom caps and add to soup. Cover and simmer over medium-low heat about 15 minutes or until mushrooms are just tender.

Garnish with fresh parsley and serve warm.
Yield: about 8 servings

HERBED BREADSTICKS

　2　packages dry yeast
　4　tablespoons sugar, divided
　1/4　cup warm water
　2　cups milk
　1/4　cup butter or margarine
　2　teaspoons salt
　6　cups all-purpose flour, divided
　1　egg white, beaten
　3　tablespoons dried Italian herb
　　　seasoning

In a small bowl, dissolve yeast and 1 tablespoon sugar in warm water; set aside. In a small saucepan, cook milk, butter, remaining 3 tablespoons sugar, and salt over medium heat until butter melts. In a large bowl, combine 5 cups flour, yeast mixture, and milk mixture; stir until a soft dough forms.

Turn onto a lightly floured surface. Adding remaining flour as needed, knead 10 to 15 minutes or until dough becomes smooth and elastic. Place in a large greased bowl, turning once to coat top of dough. Cover and let rise in a warm place (80 to 85 degrees) 1 hour or until doubled in size.

Turn dough onto a lightly floured surface and punch down. Divide dough in half. Shape half of dough into 12 equal pieces. Roll each piece into a 15-inch-long rope. Twist each rope of dough several times. Place breadsticks on a well-greased baking sheet. Repeat with remaining dough. Cover and let rise in a warm place 20 to 30 minutes or until dough rises slightly.

Preheat oven to 400 degrees. Lightly brush breadsticks with beaten egg white and sprinkle with herb seasoning. Bake about 15 minutes or until golden brown. Serve warm or transfer to a wire rack to cool.
Yield: 2 dozen breadsticks

BLOOD ORANGE SORBET

Blood oranges have red meat and are available in a limited supply from November to July.

4   cups blood orange juice (about 8 to 10 blood oranges) **or** another variety of juice orange
1   cup sugar
2   teaspoons grated blood orange zest
    Blood orange segments and mint leaves to garnish

In a medium bowl, combine orange juice, sugar, and orange zest; stir until sugar has dissolved. Chill mixture. Freeze mixture in a 2-quart ice-cream freezer according to manufacturer's instructions. To serve, garnish with orange segments and mint leaves.
Yield: about 20 servings

PEAR AND BLUE CHEESE SALAD WITH TOASTED WALNUT DRESSING

Salad may be prepared ahead of time and refrigerated; prepare dressing immediately before serving.

SALAD
8   to 10 cups mixed salad greens
1   small red onion, thinly sliced
2   red pears, quartered, cored, and thinly sliced (dip pears in a mixture of 3 tablespoons **each** water and lemon juice)

DRESSING
1   cup coarsely chopped walnuts
¹/₂   cup vegetable oil
6   tablespoons red wine vinegar
1   teaspoon sugar
¹/₂   teaspoon salt
¹/₈   teaspoon ground white pepper
4   ounces Gorgonzola cheese

For salad, arrange salad greens and onion and pear slices on 8 salad plates. Cover and refrigerate until ready to serve.

For dressing, toast walnuts in oil over medium heat in a heavy medium

Blood Orange Sorbet (top) *combines three simple ingredients for an icy-sweet treat between courses. Thin red pear slices, crumbled cheese, and onion are nestled on a bed of mixed salad greens for our deliciously tangy Pear and Blue Cheese Salad with Toasted Walnut Dressing.*

skillet about 5 minutes or until lightly browned. Reserving oil in skillet, place walnuts on a paper towel to drain. Add vinegar, sugar, salt, and white pepper to oil in skillet; stir over medium heat until well blended. Spoon dressing over salads and sprinkle with toasted walnuts and crumbled cheese.
Yield: 8 servings

93

SMOKED CORNISH HENS WITH RED CURRANT SAUCE

- 1 jar (10 ounces) red currant jelly
- 1/4 cup dry white wine
- 2 tablespoons orange juice
- 1/2 teaspoon ground allspice
- 1/8 teaspoon salt
- 1/8 teaspoon ground black pepper
- 4 Cornish hens, smoked, halved, and chilled

Preheat oven to 275 degrees. Combine jelly, wine, orange juice, allspice, salt, and pepper in a food processor. Process until well blended. Place hens in a single layer in a deep roasting pan. Baste with jelly mixture. Cover and heat in the same oven with Stuffed Deviled Onions 1 1/2 to 2 hours or until temperature registers 165 degrees on a meat thermometer. Baste hens with jelly mixture while baking. Serve warm.
Yield: 8 servings

Note: If not used as part of a progressive dinner, heat hens in a 350-degree oven 45 minutes or until heated through; baste frequently.

WHOLE GREEN BEANS WITH DILLED BUTTER CURLS

Make butter curls several hours before serving.

- 1/2 cup butter, softened
- 2 tablespoons chopped fresh dill weed **or** 1 teaspoon dried dill weed
- 1 teaspoon lemon juice
- 1 teaspoon minced onion
- 3 cans (14 1/2 ounces each) vertical pack whole green beans

In a small bowl, combine butter, dill weed, lemon juice, and onion. Shape mixture into a stick of butter slightly wider than a butter curler. Wrap in plastic wrap and chill until firm.

To prepare butter curls, dip butter curler in warm water. Pull curler across surface of seasoned butter to make

Succulent Smoked Cornish Hens are basted with flavorful Red Currant Sauce. Whole Green Beans with Dilled Butter Curls and Stuffed Deviled Onions are the perfect side dishes to complete this delightful entrée.

each curl. Place curls in ice water. Store in refrigerator until ready to serve.

Pour 3/4 cup green bean liquid into a large saucepan over medium-high heat. Place vegetable steamer in saucepan. Drain remaining liquid from green beans. Place green beans in steamer; cover and steam until heated through. Serve warm with chilled butter curls.
Yield: about 8 servings

STUFFED DEVILED ONIONS

- 8 whole white onions (about 3 inches in diameter)
- 2 tablespoons olive oil
- 2 cloves garlic, minced
- 8 medium fresh mushrooms, finely chopped
- 1/3 cup Dijon-style mustard
- 1/4 cup white wine
- 3/4 cup chicken broth, divided
- 1/2 teaspoon hot pepper sauce
- 3/4 cup (3 ounces) shredded Cheddar cheese
- 1 package (8 ounces) seasoned corn bread stuffing

Cut a small slice from bottom of each onion to flatten. Cut an "X" in bottom of each onion about 1/4-inch deep. In a Dutch oven, cook onions in boiling water 15 minutes. Drain onions; allow to cool enough to handle. Make a thin slice across top to level and scoop out center of each onion, leaving a 1/2-inch shell; reserve onion centers. Finely chop reserved onion centers to yield 1/2 cup.

Preheat oven to 275 degrees. Stirring frequently, cook oil, garlic, and chopped onion in a large saucepan over medium heat until onion is almost soft but not brown. Add mushrooms and continue to cook 2 to 3 minutes or until mushrooms are soft. Add mustard, wine, 1/4 cup chicken broth, and hot pepper sauce; stir until well blended. Remove from heat. Stir in cheese and corn bread stuffing. Fill each onion with stuffing mixture. Place onions in a 9 x 13-inch baking dish. In a microwave-safe cup, microwave remaining 1/2 cup chicken broth on high power (100%) 1 minute. Pour broth into baking dish. Cover and bake in the same oven with Smoked Cornish Hens 1 1/2 to 2 hours. Serve warm.
Yield: 8 servings

Note: If not used as part of a progressive dinner, cover and bake onions in a 350-degree oven 45 minutes or until heated through.

Bavarian Creams with Raspberry Sauce (in cups) *have a sprinkling of chocolate shavings. A decorative mold gives our Steamed Cranberry Pudding* (recipe on page 96) *its elegant shape. Laced with brandied raisins, cranberries, and toasted pecans, it's especially sumptuous served with creamy Orange Hard Sauce.*

BAVARIAN CREAMS WITH RASPBERRY SAUCE

CUSTARD
- 1 envelope unflavored gelatin
- 1/3 cup cold orange juice
- 3/4 cup sugar
- 4 egg yolks
- 1/8 teaspoon salt
- 1 3/4 cups milk, scalded
- 1 cup whipping cream

RASPBERRY SAUCE
- 1 tablespoon cornstarch
- 2 tablespoons cold water
- 1 package (12 ounces) frozen red raspberries, partially thawed
- 1/2 cup raspberry jelly
- 1 tablespoon orange-flavored liqueur
  Shaved bittersweet chocolate to garnish

For custard, soften gelatin in orange juice in a small bowl. Combine sugar, egg yolks, and salt in a small bowl; beat until well blended. Whisking constantly, add egg mixture to scalded milk in a heavy medium saucepan.

Stirring constantly, cook over medium-low heat about 20 minutes or until custard thickens enough to coat the back of a spoon. Stir gelatin mixture into hot custard, stirring until well blended. Pour custard into a medium bowl; cover and chill 1 1/2 hours.

Beat whipping cream until soft peaks form; fold into chilled custard. Spoon into individual serving dishes; cover and chill 30 minutes.

For raspberry sauce, combine cornstarch and cold water in a small bowl. In a heavy medium saucepan, combine raspberries and jelly. Bring to a boil over medium-high heat. Stirring constantly, add cornstarch mixture; stir until thickened. Press raspberry mixture through a sieve into a medium bowl; discard seeds and pulp. Stir liqueur into raspberry sauce; spoon over custard. Garnish with shaved chocolate.
Yield: about 8 servings

Our Spicy Christmas Trees are a yummy after-dinner snack. Their old-fashioned gingerbread taste is sure to please! Serve these soft cookies with Hot Fruited Tea — a heartwarming concoction of sweetened fruit juices and spiced tea.

STEAMED CRANBERRY PUDDING WITH ORANGE HARD SAUCE

(Shown on page 95)

ORANGE HARD SAUCE

- 1/2 cup butter, softened
- 1 1/2 cups sifted confectioners sugar
- 1 1/2 tablespoons brandy
- 2 teaspoons grated orange zest
- 1 teaspoon orange extract
- 1/2 teaspoon vanilla extract

CRANBERRY PUDDING

- 1 cup raisins
- 1/2 cup brandy
- 1/2 cup butter or margarine, softened
- 1/2 cup granulated sugar
- 1/2 cup firmly packed brown sugar
- 1 cup whole berry cranberry sauce
- 2 eggs
- 3/4 teaspoon butter flavoring
- 2 cups all-purpose flour
- 1 1/2 teaspoons baking powder
- 1 teaspoon ground cinnamon
- 1/2 teaspoon ground allspice
- 1/2 teaspoon baking soda
- 1/2 teaspoon salt
- 1 cup coarsely chopped fresh cranberries
- 3/4 cup finely chopped toasted pecans

For orange hard sauce, cream butter in a medium bowl. Gradually add remaining ingredients while continuing to beat; beat until fluffy. Spoon into serving dish and chill.

For cranberry pudding, combine raisins and brandy in a small saucepan over medium-low heat. Heat 5 minutes; remove from heat and set aside. In a large bowl, cream butter and sugars. Add cranberry sauce, eggs, and butter flavoring; beat until smooth. In a small bowl, combine flour, baking powder, cinnamon, allspice, baking soda, and salt. Add dry ingredients to creamed mixture; stir until well blended. Stir in cranberries, pecans, and brandied raisin mixture. Spoon batter into a greased and floured 8-cup pudding mold. Cover with mold

lid or aluminum foil. Set mold on a rack inside a large stockpot. Add boiling water to stockpot to come halfway up sides of mold. Cover stockpot and keep water at a gentle boil, adding boiling water as necessary. Steam 2 to 2$\frac{1}{4}$ hours or until a toothpick inserted in center comes out clean. Unmold steamed pudding onto serving plate and serve warm with orange hard sauce.
Yield: about 14 servings

HOT FRUITED TEA

 1 whole orange
10 cups water
 4 regular-size tea bags
 2 cinnamon sticks
 1 teaspoon whole cloves
 2 cans (12 ounces each) frozen cranberry-raspberry-strawberry juice beverage concentrate
 1 cup firmly packed brown sugar
    Orange slices to serve

Peel whole orange in one continuous strip; set peel aside and reserve orange meat for another use. Place water, tea bags, cinnamon sticks, cloves, and orange peel in a heavy large saucepan. Bring to a simmer over medium-high heat. Cover and continue to simmer 15 minutes. Strain tea into a Dutch oven; discard tea bags, orange peel, and spices. Add concentrate and brown sugar; stir over medium-low heat until sugar dissolves and tea is hot. Serve hot with orange slices.
Yield: about seventeen 6-ounce servings

SPICY CHRISTMAS TREES

COOKIES
$\frac{1}{3}$ cup butter or margarine, softened
$\frac{1}{3}$ cup vegetable shortening
1$\frac{1}{4}$ cups sugar
 1 cup sour cream
$\frac{1}{2}$ cup molasses
 2 eggs
 1 teaspoon vanilla extract
5$\frac{1}{4}$ cups all-purpose flour
$\frac{1}{4}$ cup cocoa
 1 tablespoon ground cinnamon
 2 teaspoons baking powder
 2 teaspoons ground ginger
 1 teaspoon ground allspice
 1 teaspoon baking soda
 1 teaspoon salt

ICING
 1 cup sifted confectioners sugar
 1 tablespoon plus 1 teaspoon milk

For cookies, cream butter, shortening, and sugar in a large bowl until fluffy. Add sour cream, molasses, eggs, and vanilla; beat until smooth. In another large bowl, combine flour, cocoa, cinnamon, baking powder, ginger, allspice, baking soda, and salt. Add half of dry ingredients to creamed mixture; stir until a soft dough forms. Stir remaining dry ingredients, 1 cup at a time, into dough; use hands if necessary to mix well. Divide dough into fourths. Wrap in plastic wrap and chill 2 hours or until dough is firm.

Preheat oven to 350 degrees. On a lightly floured surface, use a floured rolling pin to roll out one fourth of dough to slightly less than $\frac{1}{4}$-inch thickness. Use 3$\frac{1}{4}$ x 4-inch and 2$\frac{1}{4}$ x 3$\frac{1}{4}$-inch Christmas tree-shaped cookie cutters to cut out cookies. Transfer to a greased baking sheet. Bake 7 to 9 minutes or until firm to the touch. Transfer cookies to a wire rack to cool. Repeat with remaining dough.

For icing, combine confectioners sugar and milk in a small bowl; stir until smooth. Spoon icing into a pastry bag fitted with a small round tip. Pipe outline onto each cookie. Allow icing to harden. Store in an airtight container.
Yield: about 7 dozen cookies

SECOND-TIME SAMPLING

If you're tired of sitting down to meal after meal of the same old post-holiday turkey, try these great-tasting "recycled" dishes! Combined with a few simple ingredients, traditional holiday fare is given delicious new flavor the second time around. Our creative recipes include hearty offerings for breakfast as well as dishes for an entire dinner, from a spreadable appetizer to scrumptious desserts.

TURKEY AND SAUSAGE GUMBO

½ cup vegetable oil
¾ cup all-purpose flour
1 package (1 pound, 2 ounces) frozen sliced okra, thawed
1 cup chopped onion
¾ cup chopped celery
¾ cup chopped green onions
½ cup chopped green pepper
2 cloves garlic, minced
6 cups turkey stock or canned chicken broth
4 cups chopped cooked turkey
1 pound smoked sausage, sliced
1 can (14½ ounces) diced tomatoes
2 teaspoons hot pepper sauce
1 teaspoon dried thyme leaves
1 teaspoon dried marjoram leaves
1 teaspoon salt
½ teaspoon ground black pepper
¼ teaspoon ground red pepper
2 bay leaves
1 package (16 ounces) frozen cooked and peeled cocktail shrimp, thawed
1 teaspoon filé powder
Cooked rice to serve

Combine oil and flour in a heavy large Dutch oven over medium heat. Stirring constantly, cook 13 to 15 minutes or until mixture forms a brown roux. Reduce heat to medium-low and stir in okra, onion, celery, green onions, green pepper, and garlic. Cook 15 minutes or until vegetables are tender. Stir in turkey stock, turkey, sausage, tomatoes, pepper sauce, thyme, marjoram, salt, black pepper, red pepper, and bay leaves. Increase heat to medium-high and bring to a boil. Reduce heat to low; cover and simmer 1 hour, stirring occasionally. Remove lid and simmer 30 minutes or until desired thickness. Remove from heat; stir in shrimp and filé powder. Remove bay leaves. Serve gumbo over rice.
Yield: about 4 quarts gumbo

Loaded with Cajun-style flavor, Turkey and Sausage Gumbo will add pizzazz to your after-Christmas dinner. Use the last of the cranberry sauce to create zippy Cranberry-Orange Barbecue Sauce (top right). It's a terrific pick-me-up for turkey or chicken! Tasty Ham Spread is perfect for topping your favorite crackers.

CRANBERRY-ORANGE BARBECUE SAUCE

This is a great basting sauce or condiment for poultry and meat.

1 cup whole berry cranberry sauce
½ cup firmly packed brown sugar
¼ cup frozen orange juice concentrate, thawed
2 tablespoons red wine vinegar
1 tablespoon prepared mustard
1 tablespoon Worcestershire sauce
½ teaspoon ground black pepper

In a medium saucepan, combine cranberry sauce, brown sugar, juice concentrate, vinegar, mustard, Worcestershire sauce, and pepper over medium heat. Stirring frequently, cook 7 minutes or until heated through.
Yield: about 1½ cups sauce

TASTY HAM SPREAD

1 package (3 ounces) cream cheese, softened
¼ cup mayonnaise
2 cups ground baked ham
2 tablespoons finely chopped sweet pickle
1 tablespoon Dijon-style mustard
1 teaspoon Worcestershire sauce
Crackers to serve

In a small bowl, beat cream cheese and mayonnaise until well blended. Stir in ham, pickle, mustard, and Worcestershire sauce. Cover and chill 1 hour. Serve ham spread with crackers.
Yield: about 2 cups spread

CHEESY VEGETABLE PIE
(Shown on page 100)

This pie is made with previously cooked vegetables, or you may substitute canned or frozen.

1 cup green beans, drained
1 cup green peas, drained
1 cup sliced carrots, drained
1 cup broccoli flowerets
½ cup whole kernel corn, drained
1 cup chopped uncooked onion
¼ cup chopped uncooked green pepper
1 clove garlic, minced
¾ teaspoon salt
¼ teaspoon ground black pepper
1 cup sour cream
1 cup (4 ounces) shredded mozzarella cheese
1 tablespoon chopped fresh parsley
1 package (15 ounces) refrigerated pie crusts, at room temperature

Preheat oven to 350 degrees. In a large bowl, combine green beans, green peas, carrots, broccoli, corn, onion, green pepper, garlic, salt, and black pepper; toss until well blended. Stir in sour cream, cheese, and parsley. Press 1 crust into bottom of a 9-inch deep-dish pie plate. Cut decorative shapes from top crust. Spoon vegetable mixture into crust. Place top crust over vegetables. Arrange cutout pieces of dough on top crust. Crimp edges of crust with a fork. Bake 60 to 65 minutes or until cheese is bubbly and crust is golden brown. If edges of crust brown too quickly, cover with strips of aluminum foil. Allow pie to stand 10 minutes before serving.
Yield: 8 to 10 servings

To finish off extra veggies, here are two great ideas. Zesty Green Bean Salad (top) has tangy zing, and Cheesy Vegetable Pie (recipe on page 99) is bubbling with yummy mozzarella cheese. Snowman-shaped cutouts add a festive touch to the crust.

ZESTY GREEN BEAN SALAD

$2/3$ cup bottled chili sauce
2 cloves garlic, minced
2 tablespoons vegetable oil
1 tablespoon chopped fresh parsley
1 tablespoon freshly squeezed lemon juice
4 cups previously cooked or canned green beans, drained
$3/4$ cup finely chopped green pepper

$1/2$ small red onion, very thinly sliced and separated into rings
Lettuce leaves
8 slices bacon, cooked and crumbled
Hard-cooked egg, sliced

In a small bowl, combine chili sauce, garlic, oil, parsley, and lemon juice; stir until well blended. In a medium bowl, combine green beans and green pepper. Pour chili sauce mixture over green bean mixture; toss until well coated. Cover and chill 2 hours.

To serve, add onion rings to salad; toss. Line a serving bowl with lettuce leaves. Spoon salad over lettuce. Sprinkle with bacon and top with egg slices.
Yield: about 10 servings

Yesterday's sweet potatoes make a tasty comeback as Nutty Sweet Potato Muffins (recipe on page 102). Another terrific breakfast treat is Eggnog French Toast. Served with our spirited maple-walnut syrup, it'll make a great start for the day.

EGGNOG FRENCH TOAST

SYRUP
- 1/2 cup sugar
- 1 tablespoon cornstarch
- 1 cup boiling water
- 1/2 cup chopped walnuts
- 1 tablespoon butter
  Dash of salt
- 1/4 cup maple syrup
- 1 tablespoon bourbon

FRENCH TOAST
- Vegetable oil
- 2 cups eggnog
- 2 eggs
- 1 teaspoon vanilla extract
- 1/2 teaspoon orange extract
- 1/4 teaspoon ground nutmeg
- 1 loaf (16 ounces) French bread, cut into 3/4-inch slices

For syrup, combine sugar and cornstarch in a heavy medium saucepan. Stirring constantly over medium heat, gradually add boiling water. Add walnuts, butter, and salt; cook about 7 minutes or until mixture thickens. Remove from heat. Stir in maple syrup and bourbon.

For French toast, heat a small amount of oil in a medium skillet over medium heat. Combine eggnog, eggs, extracts, and nutmeg in a medium bowl. Dip each bread slice into eggnog mixture. Cook bread slices until each side is lightly browned. Add additional oil to skillet as necessary. Serve warm with warm syrup.

Yield: about 7 servings

101

DELIGHTFUL DESSERTS

*S*umptuous desserts are as essential to holiday festivities as mistletoe and holly. Set the stage for successful gatherings, from open houses to cozy coffees, with our impressive array of delicious tortes, pies, cakes, and more! Kissed with homemade goodness, our offerings range from an elegant floating dessert and a traditional Yule log to a chocolate-pecan tart that gives you tradition with a twist. Whether your family and friends prefer tried-and-true recipes or brand-new dishes, you'll find interesting offerings to grace your Yuletide table in this collection of yummy treats.

Swirls of spun sugar create a colorful crown for Brandy Pound Cake (recipe on page 106). Beneath the fanciful topping, you'll find a fine-textured cake that's spicy and spirited.

BRANDY POUND CAKE WITH SPUN SUGAR

(Shown on pages 104 and 105)

CAKE

1	cup butter or margarine, softened
1¹/₂	cups sugar
5	eggs
2	tablespoons brandy
1	tablespoon vanilla extract
1¹/₂	cups all-purpose flour
2	teaspoons ground ginger
1	teaspoon baking powder
¹/₂	teaspoon baking soda
¹/₂	teaspoon ground nutmeg
¹/₄	teaspoon ground mace
¹/₄	teaspoon salt

ICING

¹/₂	cup water
2	tablespoons light corn syrup
6¹/₂	cups sifted confectioners sugar
1	teaspoon vanilla extract
20	red hard candies for spun sugar

Preheat oven to 325 degrees. For cake, cream butter and sugar in a large bowl until fluffy. Add eggs, 1 at a time, beating well after each addition. Beat in brandy and vanilla. Sift flour, ginger, baking powder, baking soda, nutmeg, mace, and salt into a medium bowl. Add dry ingredients to creamed mixture; beat until well blended. Pour batter into a greased and floured 10-inch tube pan. Bake 1 hour to 1 hour 5 minutes, testing for doneness with a toothpick. Cool in pan 15 minutes; remove from pan. Cool completely on a wire rack with waxed paper underneath.

For icing, combine water and corn syrup in a medium saucepan. Stir in confectioners sugar until well blended. Attach candy thermometer to pan, making sure thermometer does not touch bottom of pan. Stirring constantly, cook over medium-low heat until icing reaches 100 degrees. Remove from heat; stir in vanilla. Cool icing 5 minutes. Ice top and sides of cake. Allow icing to harden.

In a small saucepan, melt candies over medium heat, stirring occasionally with a fork. When syrup begins to form

a thread, remove from heat. Dip fork into syrup and allow threads of syrup to fall onto a piece of ungreased aluminum foil, forming a 10-inch-diameter circle. Reheating syrup as necessary, repeat procedure with remaining syrup to form several layers of spun sugar. Allow spun sugar to harden; place on cake. Store in an airtight container.

Yield: about 16 servings

HAZELNUT TORTE

TORTE

2¹/₂	cups whole unsalted hazelnuts
4	eggs
³/₄	cup sugar
¹/₂	cup butter or margarine, melted
¹/₃	cup light corn syrup
¹/₄	cup milk
2	teaspoons vanilla extract
1¹/₄	cups all-purpose flour
1	teaspoon baking powder
¹/₂	teaspoon salt
¹/₄	teaspoon baking soda
¹/₄	teaspoon ground cinnamon

FILLING

1	package (3 ounces) vanilla pudding mix
1¹/₂	cups milk
¹/₂	cup amaretto

BUTTERCREAM FROSTING

4	cups sifted confectioners sugar
1	cup butter or margarine, softened
3	tablespoons milk
1	teaspoon vanilla extract

DECORATIVE FROSTING

¹/₃	cup water
2	tablespoons meringue powder
6	cups sifted confectioners sugar
1¹/₄	cups vegetable shortening
1	teaspoon vanilla extract
	Green paste food coloring
	Small red cinnamon candies

Preheat oven to 350 degrees. For torte, spread hazelnuts on an ungreased baking sheet. Bake 8 to

10 minutes or until nuts are slightly darker in color. Cool completely on pan. Process hazelnuts in a food processor until finely ground; set aside.

In a large bowl, beat eggs at medium speed of an electric mixer 5 minutes. Continue beating 5 minutes longer while adding sugar, 1 tablespoon at a time. Beat in melted butter, corn syrup, milk, and vanilla. Sift flour, baking powder, salt, baking soda, and cinnamon into a medium bowl. Add dry ingredients to egg mixture; beat at low speed until moistened. Stir in hazelnuts. Pour batter into 2 greased and floured 9-inch round cake pans. Bake 25 to 30 minutes or until cake begins to pull away from sides of pan and top springs back when lightly pressed. Cool in pans 15 minutes; remove from pans. Cool on a wire rack. Slice each layer in half horizontally. Separate layers with waxed paper; cover and freeze until firm.

For filling, combine pudding mix and milk in a medium saucepan. Stirring constantly, cook over medium heat until mixture comes to a rolling boil. Stir in amaretto; bring to a boil. Transfer to a small heat-resistant bowl. Cover and refrigerate until well chilled. Spread filling between cake layers.

For buttercream frosting, combine all ingredients in a large bowl; beat until smooth. Frost sides and top of cake. Transfer remaining frosting to a pastry bag fitted with a small star tip. Pipe a decorative border along bottom edge of cake.

For decorative frosting, combine water and meringue powder in a medium bowl; beat until soft peaks form. Add 2 cups confectioners sugar, beating until well blended. Alternately add shortening and remaining 4 cups confectioners sugar; beat until well blended. Beat in vanilla. Tint frosting green. Transfer frosting to a pastry bag fitted with a large leaf tip (we used tip #112). Pipe leaves on top of cake for wreath design. Place candies on leaves. Cover and store in refrigerator.

Yield: about 20 servings

An impressive holly wreath fashioned from frosting and candies transforms Hazelnut Torte into a festive centerpiece. The tempting dessert is made by spooning a delicious vanilla pudding filling laced with amaretto between thin layers of delicate, nutty cake. Buttercream frosting completes the treat.

FLOATING HOLIDAY DESSERT

DESSERT

- 3/4 cup sugar
- 1/3 cup water
- 3 egg yolks
  Dash salt
- 1 cup crumbled coconut macaroons
- 5 ladyfingers, split
- 2 tablespoons brandy
- 1 1/2 cups whipping cream
- 2 teaspoons vanilla extract
- 1/2 teaspoon almond extract

RASPBERRY SAUCE

- 1/2 cup sugar
- 1/4 cup water
- 1 package (10 ounces) frozen red raspberries, thawed
- 2 tablespoons lemon juice
- 2 tablespoons raspberry-flavored liqueur
- 2 teaspoons cornstarch
- 3 teaspoons water

For dessert, combine sugar and water in a small saucepan. Bring to a boil over medium heat and stir until sugar is dissolved. Continue to gently boil, without stirring, until mixture reaches 230 degrees on a candy thermometer. Sugar mixture will spin a thread when dropped from spoon. Remove from heat.

In a large bowl, beat egg yolks and salt until light in color. Gradually add hot syrup, pouring in a thin stream; beat until mixture begins to cool (about 2 minutes). Stir in macaroons. Place mixture in refrigerator 30 minutes.

Sprinkle ladyfingers with brandy; cover and set aside. In a small bowl, combine whipping cream and extracts; beat until stiff peaks form. Fold whipped cream into chilled mixture. Place half of mixture into an oiled 6-cup ring mold. Cover with ladyfingers; top with remaining mixture. Cover tightly and freeze until firm (about 4 hours).

For raspberry sauce, combine sugar and water in a medium saucepan. Bring to a boil over medium heat; stir until sugar is dissolved. Boil 2 minutes and remove from heat. Add raspberries, lemon juice, and liqueur. Return to heat and cook until well blended, stirring constantly. In a small bowl, dissolve cornstarch in water. Stir cornstarch mixture into raspberry mixture; cook until thickened. Remove from heat and cool. Store in an airtight container in refrigerator until ready to serve.

To serve, dip mold into hot water to loosen ring. Invert onto a chilled shallow serving dish. Spoon raspberry sauce around dessert and serve.
Yield: 10 servings

FRUITY PUDDING CAKE

Enjoy the convenience of packaged mixes in this holiday dessert.

- 2 packages (3 3/4 ounces each) vanilla pudding mix and milk to prepare pudding
- 1 package (18 1/4 ounces) pineapple cake mix and ingredients to prepare cake
- 1 container (4 ounces) red candied cherries
- 1 can (8 3/4 ounces) crushed pineapple in heavy syrup, drained
- 1/2 cup chopped dates
- 1/2 cup canned apricot halves, drained and chopped
- 1/2 cup flaked coconut
- 8 tablespoons brandy, divided
- 3/4 cup chopped pecans
- 2 cups whipping cream, whipped

Prepare pudding according to package directions. Cool completely and chill in the refrigerator several hours.

Preheat oven to 350 degrees. Prepare cake mix according to package directions. Pour batter into a greased and floured 11 x 17-inch jellyroll pan. Bake 18 to 22 minutes or until center is firm when touched. Cool on a wire rack.

Reserve 10 cherries to garnish. Chop remaining cherries. Combine chopped cherries, pineapple, dates, apricots, and coconut. Spoon 2 tablespoons brandy over mixture; drain. Combine fruit mixture with cold pudding. Stir in pecans. Return mixture to refrigerator until ready to assemble cake.

Cut cake in half (you will have two 8 1/2 x 11-inch pieces). Sprinkle remaining 6 tablespoons brandy over bottom layer of cake. Spread pudding mixture over cake; place remaining layer of cake on top. Spread whipped cream over top. Cut into 2-inch squares. Cut reserved cherries in half; garnish each square with a cherry piece.
Yield: 20 servings

Cap off your Yuletide fete with eye-catching yummies that will be long remembered. Floating Holiday Dessert (lower left) features brandied ladyfingers nestled in a tempting coconut concoction. This molded delicacy is elegantly displayed on a bed of liqueur-tinged Raspberry Sauce. Another tasty attraction, pineapple-flavored Fruity Pudding Cake (right) is highlighted with nuts, fruits, and vanilla pudding.

COCONUT SNOWBALL

CAKE

- 1 package (18¼ ounces) white cake mix with pudding in the mix
- 1 can (18½ ounces) cream of coconut
- 1 container (8 ounces) sour cream
- 3 eggs
- ¼ cup vegetable oil

FROSTING

- 1 package (6 ounces) white baking chocolate, coarsely chopped
- 4 cups confectioners sugar
- ½ cup evaporated milk
- 2 cups flaked coconut

Preheat oven to 350 degrees. For cake, combine cake mix, cream of coconut, sour cream, eggs, and oil in a large bowl; beat until smooth. Pour into a well-greased and floured 10-cup ovenproof glass bowl. Bake 45 to 50 minutes or until a toothpick inserted in center of cake comes out clean. Cool in bowl 15 minutes. Remove cake from bowl and cool completely on a wire rack. Cover and chill 1 hour.

For frosting, melt chocolate in top of a double boiler over simmering water. Transfer to a large bowl. Beat in confectioners sugar and evaporated milk. Place chilled cake on a serving plate. Spread frosting over cake. Sprinkle coconut over cake. Store in refrigerator.

Yield: 12 to 14 servings

YULE LOG

In France this delicate cake is known as a Bûche de Noël.

CAKE

- 1 cup all-purpose flour
- 1¼ teaspoons baking soda
- ¼ teaspoon salt
- 6 tablespoons cocoa
- ⅓ cup boiling water
- 1½ teaspoons vanilla extract
- ¼ cup butter, softened
- 1 cup granulated sugar, divided
- 3 eggs, separated
- ¼ cup buttermilk
- 1 tablespoon confectioners sugar

CREAM FILLING

- 1 cup whipping cream
- ½ cup sugar
- 1½ teaspoons vanilla extract

GLAZE

- 1 package (12 ounces) semisweet chocolate chips
- ½ cup butter, softened
- ½ cup whipping cream
  Confectioners sugar
  Artificial holly to decorate

Preheat oven to 325 degrees. For cake, grease a 10½ x 15½-inch jellyroll pan. Line bottom of pan with waxed paper; grease and flour waxed paper. In a small bowl, combine flour, baking soda, and salt. In another small bowl, whisk cocoa, water, and vanilla until smooth.

In a large bowl, cream butter. Gradually beat in ¾ cup plus 2 tablespoons granulated sugar. Beat in egg yolks, 1 at a time, beating well after each addition. Beat until mixture is light and fluffy, about 2 to 3 minutes. Alternately beat flour mixture and buttermilk into creamed mixture. Beat in cocoa mixture until well blended. In a medium bowl beat egg whites until soft peaks form. Gradually beat in remaining 2 tablespoons granulated sugar until stiff peaks form. Fold egg white mixture into chocolate mixture. Pour batter into prepared pan. Bake 12 to 15 minutes until cake is slightly puffed and just begins to pull away from sides of pan. Sift confectioners sugar onto a towel. Loosen sides of cake and invert onto towel. Remove waxed paper. Beginning with 1 long edge, roll cake in towel. Cool cake 45 minutes or until room temperature.

For cream filling, beat whipping cream, sugar, and vanilla in a large bowl until stiff peaks form. Unroll cake and remove towel. Spread filling over cake to within 1 inch of edges. Beginning at 1 long edge, roll up cake jellyroll style. Wrap tightly in aluminum foil and freeze overnight.

For glaze, melt chocolate chips in top of a double boiler over warm water. Remove from heat and cool slightly. Beat in butter and whipping cream until slightly thickened. Remove cake from freezer; unwrap. Place cake, seam side down, on a wire rack with waxed paper underneath. Spread glaze over top and sides of cake. Transfer to serving platter. Gently pull a fork through glaze to form "bark" lines. Refrigerate until ready to serve. To serve, sift confectioners sugar over cake. Decorate with holly.

Yield: 10 to 12 servings

Rich through and through, our Coconut Snowball (top) *is a moist coconut cake blanketed with luscious white chocolate frosting and sprinkled with shredded coconut. Chocolate Yule Log* (bottom), *a traditional French Christmas dessert, is another eye-pleasing dish.*

OLD-FASHIONED MINTS

1/4 cup butter or margarine
3 3/4 cups sifted confectioners sugar, divided
1/3 cup light corn syrup
1/2 teaspoon peppermint extract
1/2 teaspoon vanilla extract
      Red paste food coloring

In a heavy medium saucepan over medium heat, melt butter. Add 2 cups confectioners sugar and corn syrup; stir until well blended. Stirring constantly, cook about 4 minutes or until mixture comes to a boil. Remove from heat and add remaining 1 3/4 cups confectioners sugar; stir about 3 minutes or until mixture thickens. Stir in extracts. Pour mixture onto a smooth, damp surface; use a spatula to knead mixture until cool enough to handle with lightly greased hands. Continue kneading until very smooth and creamy. Divide mixture in half, wrapping one half in plastic wrap. Tint remaining half red. Using a rolling pin, quickly roll red mixture into a 5 x 18-inch rectangle on plastic wrap. Cover with plastic wrap. Repeat to roll out white mixture; place over red layer. Beginning at 1 long edge, tightly roll up layers. Using a serrated knife with a sawing motion, carefully cut roll into 3/8-inch slices. Store in an airtight container in a cool place.

Yield: about 4 dozen mints

ALMOND-POPPY SEED ANGEL FOOD CAKE

1 package (16 ounces) angel food cake mix
2 tablespoons poppy seed
1 1/2 teaspoons almond extract, divided
1 1/2 cups sifted confectioners sugar
2 tablespoons water
1/4 cup sliced almonds

Preheat oven to 350 degrees. Prepare cake mix according to package directions, stirring in poppy seed and 1 teaspoon almond extract. Pour into an ungreased 10-inch tube pan. Bake 40 to 45 minutes or until top is golden brown. Invert pan; cool completely.

Transfer cake to a serving plate. Combine confectioners sugar, water, and remaining 1/2 teaspoon almond extract in a small bowl. Drizzle glaze over cake; sprinkle with almonds.

Yield: 16 servings

1 serving: 202 calories, 1.3 grams fat, 3.6 grams protein, 44.1 grams carbohydrate

CALICO PIE

We used the scraps of dough and miniature cookie cutters to cut out little dogs and cats to decorate the edge and center of the pie. Just bake the cutouts separately 5 to 10 minutes. When the pie is cool, use a little corn syrup to "glue" the cutouts around the edge.

CRUST

2 1/4 cups all-purpose flour
1/2 teaspoon salt
3/4 cup plus 2 tablespoons chilled butter, cut into pieces
1/3 cup ice water

FILLING

1 1/2 cups sugar
1 cup golden raisins
1 1/2 cups peeled, cored, and chopped apple
1 cup whole berry cranberry sauce
3 tablespoons lemon juice
1/2 teaspoon salt
1/2 teaspoon ground cinnamon
1/4 teaspoon ground cloves
1/4 teaspoon ground ginger

Preheat oven to 400 degrees. For crust, sift flour and salt into a medium bowl. Using a pastry blender or 2 knives, cut in butter until mixture resembles coarse meal. Sprinkle water over dough, mixing quickly just until dough forms a ball (dough will be soft). Divide dough in half. On a lightly floured surface, use a floured rolling pin to roll out one half of dough. Place the dough in an ungreased 9-inch pie pan. Roll out remaining half of dough. If using miniature cookie cutters, cut holes in center of top crust; set aside.

For filling, combine sugar, raisins, apple, cranberry sauce, lemon juice, salt, cinnamon, cloves, and ginger in a medium bowl. Pour into pie shell. Top pie with remaining dough. Trim and crimp edges of pie. If not using miniature cookie cutters, cut slits in top of pie for steam to escape. Bake 35 to 40 minutes or until crust is golden brown. Serve warm or at room temperature.

Yield: 8 servings

Superb as after-dinner treats, Old-Fashioned Mints (clockwise from top left) are soft, buttery pinwheels that taste just like the ones Grandmother made. Drizzled with glaze and topped with sliced almonds, Almond-Poppy Seed Angel Food Cake is an inviting dessert with added appeal for the calorie conscious! Tart cranberry-apple Calico Pie gets its country charm from the parade of animal cutouts that decorate its crust.

ULTIMATE CHOCOLATE PUDDING

3 ounces semisweet baking chocolate, coarsely chopped
3 ounces unsweetened baking chocolate, coarsely chopped
1/4 cup butter or margarine
3 cups milk
1 1/4 cups sugar, divided
2 eggs
4 egg yolks
1/2 cup cocoa
2 teaspoons cornstarch
2 cups whipping cream, divided
1 teaspoon vanilla extract
1 tablespoon finely chopped bittersweet baking chocolate and fresh mint leaves to garnish

In top of a double boiler over simmering water, melt chocolates and butter, stirring until well blended. Remove from heat and allow to cool. In a heavy large saucepan over medium heat, whisk milk, 1 cup sugar, eggs, and egg yolks. Attach a candy thermometer to pan, making sure thermometer does not touch bottom of pan. Stirring constantly, cook until mixture reaches 180 degrees on candy thermometer or begins to thicken. Strain custard through a fine-mesh strainer into a large bowl. In a heavy small saucepan, sift cocoa and cornstarch into 1 cup whipping cream. Stirring constantly, bring mixture to a boil; cook until slightly thickened. Add chocolate mixture, cornstarch mixture, and vanilla to custard; stir until well blended. Pour into individual serving dishes; cover and chill.

To serve, chill a small bowl and beaters from an electric mixer in freezer. In chilled bowl, beat remaining 1 cup whipping cream and remaining 1/4 cup sugar until stiff peaks form. Spoon mixture into a pastry bag fitted with a large star tip. Pipe whipped cream mixture onto pudding. Garnish with chopped bittersweet chocolate and mint leaves.

Yield: 8 to 10 servings

Four kinds of chocolate are used to create our creamy Ultimate Chocolate Pudding (top). *Packed with pecans, Penuche is a delightful brown sugar fudge.*

PENUCHE

2 cups firmly packed brown sugar
2/3 cup half and half
1 1/2 tablespoons light corn syrup
1/8 teaspoon salt
2 tablespoons butter or margarine, softened
1 teaspoon vanilla extract
1 cup chopped pecans

Line a 7 x 11-inch baking pan with aluminum foil, extending foil over ends of pan; butter foil. Butter sides of a heavy large saucepan. Combine brown sugar, half and half, corn syrup, and salt in saucepan. Stirring constantly, cook over medium-low heat until sugar dissolves. Using a pastry brush dipped in hot water, wash down any sugar crystals on sides of pan. Attach a candy thermometer to pan, making sure thermometer does not touch bottom of pan. Increase heat to medium and bring to a boil. Cook, without stirring, until syrup reaches soft-ball stage (approximately 234 to 240 degrees). Test about 1/2 teaspoon syrup in ice water. Syrup will easily form a ball in ice water but will flatten when held in your hand. Place pan in cold water in sink. Cool, without stirring, to approximately 110 degrees. Add butter and vanilla. Using an electric mixer, beat fudge until thickened and no longer glossy. Stir in pecans. Pour mixture into prepared pan. Cool completely. Use ends of foil to lift fudge from pan. Cut into 1-inch squares.

Yield: about 5 dozen pieces fudge

CHOCOLATE FRUITCAKE

CAKE

- 1/2 cup butter
- 1/2 cup granulated sugar
- 1/2 cup firmly packed brown sugar
- 2 eggs
- 1 teaspoon vanilla extract
- 1/2 cup buttermilk
- 4 ounces semisweet baking chocolate, melted
- 2 1/2 cups all-purpose flour
- 1 teaspoon baking powder
- 1 teaspoon baking soda
- 1 teaspoon salt
- 3/4 cup cherry preserves
- 1/4 cup brandy
- 1 cup chopped red candied cherries
- 1 cup chopped dates
- 1 cup coarsely chopped pecans

GLAZE

- 1/4 cup water
- 1 1/2 tablespoons cornstarch
- 1/2 cup sugar
- 3 tablespoons cocoa
- 2 1/2 tablespoons butter
- 2 tablespoons brandy
- 1/2 teaspoon vanilla extract
  Candied cherry and pecan halves to decorate

Preheat oven to 350 degrees. For cake, cream butter and sugars in a large bowl. Add eggs and vanilla; beat until smooth. Stir in buttermilk and melted chocolate. In a medium bowl, combine flour, baking powder, baking soda, and salt. Add dry ingredients to creamed mixture; stir until well blended. Add preserves and brandy; stir until well blended. Stir in cherries, dates, and pecans. Spoon batter into a well-greased 10-inch fluted tube pan. Bake 50 to 60 minutes or until a toothpick inserted in center of cake comes out clean. Cool in pan 10 minutes. Invert cake onto a serving plate.

For glaze, combine water and cornstarch in a small saucepan; stir until cornstarch dissolves. Stir in sugar and cocoa. Stirring frequently, cook over medium heat until mixture begins

Flavored with semisweet chocolate, spirited Chocolate Fruitcake is like the traditional holiday favorite — only better! A decadent brandy-laced chocolate glaze covers the cake, which is garnished with candied cherries and pecan halves.

to boil; add butter, brandy, and vanilla. Remove from heat and stir until butter melts; allow glaze to cool 5 minutes. Pour glaze over warm cake. Decorate with cherry and pecan halves. Cool completely. Store in an airtight container.

Yield: about 16 servings

WHITE CHOCOLATE PROFITEROLES

CREAM PUFF PASTRY
1 cup plus 1 teaspoon water, divided
1/2 cup butter or margarine
1 cup all-purpose flour
4 eggs
1 egg
1/8 teaspoon salt

FILLING
1 3/4 cups whipping cream, divided
1/3 cup sugar
4 ounces white chocolate, chopped
1/8 teaspoon salt

TOPPING
3 ounces white chocolate, chopped
Red and green paste food coloring

Preheat oven to 400 degrees. For cream puff pastry, bring 1 cup water and butter to a boil in a heavy large saucepan over high heat. Remove from heat. Add flour all at once; stir with a wooden spoon until mixture forms a ball. Place flour mixture in a medium bowl. Add 4 eggs, 1 at a time, beating well with an electric mixer after each addition. Spoon batter into a pastry bag fitted with a large round tip (1/2-inch opening). Placing 2 inches apart on a greased and floured baking sheet, pipe 1 1/2-inch-diameter by 1-inch-high puffs. In a small bowl, whisk 1 egg, remaining 1 teaspoon water, and salt until well blended. Brush egg wash over tops of puffs, gently rounding out tops. Bake puffs 10 minutes in upper one-third of oven. Reduce heat to 350 degrees; bake 25 to 30 minutes longer or until puffs are firm to the touch and golden. Transfer puffs to a wire rack and cool completely.

For filling, chill a medium bowl and beaters from an electric mixer in freezer. Combine 1/4 cup whipping cream and sugar in top of a double boiler. Stirring frequently, cook over simmering water until sugar dissolves. Stirring constantly, add white chocolate and salt; continue to cook until chocolate melts. Remove from heat; allow mixture to cool. In chilled bowl, beat remaining 1 1/2 cups whipping cream until stiff peaks form; gradually add chocolate mixture while continuing to beat. Chill until ready to fill puffs.

For topping, melt white chocolate in top of a double boiler over simmering water. Divide melted chocolate into 2 small bowls; tint red and green. Spoon chocolate into separate pastry bags fitted with small round tips. To serve, slice puffs in half horizontally with a sharp serrated knife; place 1 1/2 tablespoons of filling between halves. Drizzle each color of chocolate over puffs.

Yield: about 2 dozen puffs

COCONUT-ORANGE SQUARES

CAKE
3/4 cup butter or margarine, softened
3/4 cup sugar
1 can (16 ounces) sliced carrots, drained and mashed
1 egg
1 1/2 teaspoons grated orange zest
1/2 teaspoon vanilla extract
1/4 teaspoon orange extract
2 cups all-purpose flour
2 teaspoons baking powder
3/4 teaspoon salt
3/4 cup flaked coconut

ICING
1 package (8 ounces) cream cheese, softened
1/4 cup butter or margarine, softened
2 teaspoons milk
1/2 teaspoon grated orange zest
1/2 teaspoon orange extract
1/4 teaspoon vanilla extract
3 1/2 cups sifted confectioners sugar
1/2 cup toasted flaked coconut to garnish

Preheat oven to 350 degrees. For cake, cream butter and sugar in a large bowl until fluffy. Add carrots, egg, orange zest, and extracts; beat until smooth. In a medium bowl, combine flour, baking powder, and salt. Add dry ingredients to creamed mixture; stir until well blended. Stir in coconut. Pour batter into a lightly greased 9 x 13-inch pan. Bake 20 to 25 minutes or until a toothpick inserted in center of cake comes out clean. Place pan on a wire rack to cool.

For icing, beat cream cheese, butter, milk, orange zest, and extracts in a medium bowl until smooth. Stir in confectioners sugar until smooth. Spread icing over cooled cake. Garnish with toasted coconut. Cut into 2-inch squares.

Yield: about 2 dozen squares

For airy White Chocolate Profiteroles (top), *fluffy white chocolate is piped into individual cream puff pastries. Sporting rich cream cheese icing and toasted coconut, Coconut-Orange Squares are moist and chewy.*

CHOCOLATE-MINT TORTE

CAKE

- ½ cup butter or margarine, softened
- 1¾ cups sugar
- 2 eggs
- 1 teaspoon vanilla extract
- 2 cups all-purpose flour
- 1 teaspoon baking powder
- 1 teaspoon baking soda
- ¼ teaspoon salt
- ¾ cup buttermilk
- ½ cup coffee-flavored liqueur
- 4 ounces unsweetened baking chocolate, melted

FILLING

- 4 egg whites
- ½ cup sugar
- 1 tablespoon water
- ¼ teaspoon cream of tartar
- ⅛ teaspoon salt
- 8 ounces semisweet baking chocolate, melted
- 1 cup whipping cream
- 2 tablespoons crème de menthe
- 15 individually wrapped chocolate wafer mints to garnish

A chocolate fancier's delight, elegant Chocolate-Mint Torte layers melt-in-your-mouth buttermilk chocolate cake with a crème de menthe filling. Curls of mint-chocolate candy embellish this exquisite offering.

Preheat oven to 350 degrees. For cake, cream butter and sugar in a large bowl until fluffy. Add eggs and vanilla; stir until smooth. Sift flour, baking powder, baking soda, and salt into a medium bowl. Alternately add buttermilk, liqueur, and dry ingredients to creamed mixture; beat until well blended. Stir in melted chocolate. Line bottoms of 3 ungreased 9-inch round cake pans with waxed paper. Divide batter evenly in pans. Bake 20 to 25 minutes or until a toothpick inserted in center of cake comes out clean. Cool in pans 10 minutes; remove from pans and cool completely on a wire rack.

For filling, chill a small bowl and beaters from an electric mixer in freezer. In top of a double boiler over simmering water, combine egg whites, sugar, water, cream of tartar, and salt. Whisking constantly, cook until mixture reaches 160 degrees on a thermometer (about 8 minutes). Transfer to a large bowl and beat until stiff peaks form. Gently fold melted chocolate into cooked mixture. In chilled bowl, beat whipping cream and créme de menthe until stiff peaks form. Gentle fold into chocolate mixture. Refrigerate until ready to use.

To assemble cake, place 1 cake layer on a cake plate; spread one-third of filling on cake layer. Repeat with remaining layers and filling. To garnish, use a vegetable peeler to shave chocolate curls from mints; place on top of cake. Cover and store in refrigerator.

Yield: about 12 servings

GINGERBREAD SQUARES

CAKE

- 1/4 cup butter or margarine, softened
- 1/2 cup sugar
- 1/2 cup sour cream
- 1/2 cup molasses
- 2 eggs
- 3/4 teaspoon vanilla extract
- 1/4 teaspoon orange extract
- 1 1/4 cups all-purpose flour
- 1/2 cup whole-wheat flour
- 1 teaspoon baking soda
- 1 teaspoon ground cinnamon
- 1 teaspoon ground ginger
- 1/2 teaspoon ground allspice
- 1/4 teaspoon salt

ICING

- 1/2 cup butter or margarine
- 1 cup firmly packed brown sugar
- 1/4 cup whipping cream
- 1 tablespoon light corn syrup
- 1 cup sifted confectioners sugar
- 1 teaspoon vanilla extract
- 1/2 cup finely chopped walnuts

Preheat oven to 350 degrees. For cake, line bottom of a greased 9-inch square baking pan with waxed paper; grease waxed paper. In a large bowl, cream butter and sugar until fluffy. Add sour cream, molasses, eggs, and extracts; beat until smooth. In a small bowl, combine flours, baking soda, cinnamon, ginger, allspice, and salt. Add dry ingredients to creamed mixture; stir until well blended. Spread batter into prepared pan. Bake 24 to 28 minutes or until a toothpick inserted in center of cake comes out clean. Cool in pan on a wire rack.

For icing, melt butter in a heavy medium saucepan over medium heat. Stirring constantly, add brown sugar, whipping cream, and corn syrup; cook until mixture comes to a boil. Boil 1 minute. Remove from heat; pour into a medium heat-resistant bowl. Add confectioners sugar and vanilla; beat until smooth. Stir in walnuts. Spread icing over cake. Cut into 2-inch squares.

Yield: about 16 servings

Our yummy Gingerbread Squares are topped with a creamy brown sugar icing that's loaded with walnuts. Aromatic Cinnamon Mocha is a perfect accompaniment for these tasty treats.

CINNAMON MOCHA

- 6 ounces semisweet baking chocolate, chopped
- 1/2 cup half and half
- 1/4 cup sugar
- 1/2 teaspoon ground cinnamon
- 1 1/2 quarts hot brewed coffee

Combine chocolate, half and half, sugar, and cinnamon in top of a double boiler over hot water; stir until chocolate melts. Transfer chocolate mixture to a large heat-resistant container. Pour brewed coffee over chocolate mixture; whisk until frothy. Pour into cups and serve hot.

Yield: about ten 6-ounce servings

SPICY CRANBERRY-NUT CAKE

CAKE
- 8 eggs
- 1 tablespoon vanilla extract
- 2 cups sugar
- 1 cup all-purpose flour
- 4 teaspoons baking powder
- 1 teaspoon ground cinnamon
- 5 cups chopped pecans

FILLING
- 1 can (8¼ ounces) crushed pineapple in heavy syrup
- 3 tablespoons cornstarch
- 1 can (16 ounces) whole berry cranberry sauce
- Red liquid food coloring

ICING
- 1½ cups whipping cream
- 2 tablespoons sifted confectioners sugar
- ¼ teaspoon ground cinnamon
- ⅛ teaspoon ground mace
- 4 pecan halves to decorate

Preheat oven to 350 degrees. For cake, grease three 9-inch round cake pans and line bottoms with waxed paper. In a large bowl, beat eggs and vanilla 5 minutes at high speed of an electric mixer. In a small bowl, combine sugar, flour, baking powder, and cinnamon. Reduce mixer to medium speed and add dry ingredients to egg mixture; beat 5 minutes. Reduce speed to low and stir in pecans. Pour batter into prepared pans. Bake 25 to 30 minutes or until a toothpick inserted in center of cake comes out clean. Cool in pans on a wire rack 5 minutes. Transfer cakes to wire rack to cool completely.

For filling, drain pineapple, reserving ¼ cup syrup. Combine syrup with cornstarch in a heavy medium saucepan. Add pineapple and cranberry sauce. Stirring constantly, cook over medium-high heat until mixture comes to a boil and thickens; reduce heat to medium and boil 2 minutes. Add 5 drops food coloring.

Transfer filling to a covered container and chill 2 hours.

For icing, place a small bowl and beaters from electric mixer in freezer to chill. Spread filling between layers and on top of cake. In chilled bowl, beat whipping cream, confectioners sugar, cinnamon, and mace until stiff peaks form. Ice sides of cake. Transfer remaining icing to a pastry bag fitted with a medium open star tip; pipe shell borders. Decorate with pecan halves and icing. Store in refrigerator until ready to serve.

Yield: about 12 servings

MULLED CRANBERRY PORT

- 4 cups cranberry juice cocktail
- 1 can (6 ounces) frozen orange juice concentrate
- ½ cup sugar
- 1 tablespoon whole cloves
- ½ teaspoon whole allspice
- 1 cinnamon stick
- 2 medium oranges, sliced
- 1 bottle (750 ml) tawny or ruby port wine
- Cinnamon sticks and orange slices to serve

Combine cranberry juice cocktail, orange juice concentrate, and sugar in a Dutch oven over medium-high heat. Place cloves and allspice in a coffee filter; tie with kitchen string and add spice bundle to juice mixture. Add cinnamon stick and orange slices. Bring to a boil. Reduce heat to low; add wine and stir until mixture is heated through. Remove spice bundle. Serve hot with additional cinnamon sticks and orange slices.

Yield: about ten 6-ounce servings

HOT FUDGE SUNDAE CAKE

- 1 cup all-purpose flour
- ¾ cup granulated sugar
- ½ cup cocoa, divided
- 2 teaspoons baking powder
- ¼ teaspoon salt
- ½ cup milk
- 2 tablespoons vegetable oil
- 1 teaspoon vanilla extract
- 1 cup firmly packed brown sugar
- 1¾ cups hot brewed coffee
- Whipped cream, chopped pecans, and maraschino cherries to serve

Preheat oven to 350 degrees. In a medium bowl, combine flour, granulated sugar, ¼ cup cocoa, baking powder, and salt. In a large bowl, combine milk, oil, and vanilla; stir in flour mixture. Spread batter into an ungreased 9-inch square baking pan; sprinkle with brown sugar and remaining ¼ cup cocoa. Slowly pour hot coffee over mixture (do not stir). Bake 35 to 40 minutes or until cake begins to crack on top and pull away from sides. Cool in pan on a wire rack 15 minutes. To serve, spoon cake into serving dishes; top with whipped cream, pecans, and cherries.

Yield: about 10 servings

Easy as pie to make, Hot Fudge Sundae Cake (top) is ready in minutes — with the fudge topping baked right in. Individual servings are garnished with whipped cream, chopped nuts, and cherries. Spicy Cranberry-Nut Cake (bottom) offers a tart filling of whole cranberries and crushed pineapple nestled between moist layers of nutty spice cake. Pecans and sweetened whipped cream touched with cinnamon and mace decorate the cake. A warm, spirited beverage, Mulled Cranberry Port is made with orange and cranberry juices, wine, and spices.

WHITE CHRISTMAS CAKES

CAKE

1 cup sugar
6 eggs
1 cup all-purpose flour
$^1/_2$ cup butter or margarine,
    melted, at room temperature
2 teaspoons almond extract

ICING

$4^1/_2$ cups granulated sugar
$2^1/_4$ cups hot water
$^1/_4$ teaspoon cream of tartar
1 teaspoon clear vanilla extract
$4^1/_2$ cups sifted confectioners sugar

ROYAL ICING

$2^1/_4$ cups sifted confectioners sugar
$1^1/_2$ tablespoons meringue powder
2 to 3 tablespoons warm water
$^1/_2$ teaspoon almond extract

Preheat oven to 350 degrees. For cake, whisk sugar and eggs in top of a double boiler over simmering water. Stirring occasionally, cook 5 to 10 minutes or until sugar dissolves. Pour mixture into a large bowl and beat with an electric mixer 10 to 12 minutes or until volume is tripled and mixture is cooled. Using low speed of electric mixer and adding $^1/_3$ cup flour at a time, sift and stir flour into egg mixture. Gently fold in melted butter and almond extract. Line a greased 9 x 13-inch baking pan with waxed paper, extending paper over ends of pan. Spread batter in pan. Bake 18 to 20 minutes or until a toothpick inserted in center of cake comes out clean. Cool cake in pan 5 minutes. Use ends of waxed paper to lift cake from pan; transfer to a wire rack. Invert onto a second wire rack and remove paper. Cool completely.

For icing, combine granulated sugar, water, and cream of tartar in a medium saucepan. Stirring constantly, cook mixture over medium-high heat until sugar dissolves. Stirring frequently, bring mixture to a boil. Reduce heat to medium. Using a pastry brush dipped in hot water, wash down any sugar crystals on sides of pan. Attach a

Kissed with almond flavor, dainty White Christmas Cakes are sumptuous tidbits that few can resist. Indulge your sweet tooth with Strawberry-Banana Frozen Yogurt. Wonderfully low in fat and calories, it's a frosty treat!

candy thermometer to pan, making sure thermometer does not touch bottom of pan. Allow mixture to boil about 15 minutes or until thermometer reaches 226 degrees, stirring only if icing begins to stick. Remove from heat and allow to cool at room temperature, without stirring, about 1 hour or until thermometer reaches 110 degrees. Add vanilla; stir in confectioners sugar until icing is a good consistency to spoon over cakes. If necessary, beat icing with an electric mixer to remove any

lumps. Cut cake into 2-inch squares. Place wire rack containing cakes over a jellyroll pan. Spoon icing over cakes. Allow icing to harden.

For royal icing, beat confectioners sugar, meringue powder, water, and almond extract in a medium bowl 7 to 10 minutes or until stiff. Spoon icing into a pastry bag fitted with a small round tip. Pipe desired decorations onto tops of cakes.
Yield: 20 cakes

STRAWBERRY-BANANA FROZEN YOGURT

- ¹/₂ cup sugar
- 1 envelope unflavored gelatin
- 1 cup cold skim milk
- 2¹/₂ cups nonfat strawberry-banana yogurt
- 1 cup puréed frozen unsweetened strawberries
- 1 banana, puréed
  Frozen or fresh strawberry slices and fresh mint leaves to garnish

In a medium saucepan, combine sugar and gelatin; add milk and allow to stand 1 minute. Stirring constantly, cook over low heat 5 minutes or until gelatin dissolves. Allow mixture to cool. Add yogurt, strawberries, and banana; stir until well blended. Freeze in an ice cream freezer according to manufacturer's instructions (or freeze overnight in an airtight container; remove from freezer, beat 5 minutes, and refreeze). To serve, garnish with strawberry slices and mint leaves.
Yield: about 1¹/₄ quarts yogurt

RING OF GOLD APRICOT CAKE

CAKE

- 1 cup butter or margarine, softened
- 2 cups sugar
- 5 eggs
- ¹/₂ cup apricot jam
- ¹/₂ cup sour cream
- 1 teaspoon vanilla extract
- 2 cups all-purpose flour
- 1 teaspoon baking soda
- ¹/₂ teaspoon salt
- 2 cups flaked coconut
- 1 cup finely chopped pecans
- 1 package (8 ounces) dried apricots, finely chopped

GLAZE

- ¹/₂ cup apricot jam
- 2 tablespoons apricot nectar

Preheat oven to 350 degrees. For cake, cream butter and sugar in a large

Sour cream and apricot jam give our Ring of Gold Apricot Cake a rich flavor and moist texture. This tube cake, named for the symbol of never-ending love, represents the enduring bond we share with special friends and relatives.

bowl until fluffy. Add eggs, 1 at a time, beating well after each addition. Stir in jam, sour cream, and vanilla. Sift flour, baking soda, and salt into a medium bowl. Stir dry ingredients into creamed mixture. Fold in coconut, pecans, and apricots. Pour batter into a greased and floured 10-inch springform pan with fluted tube insert. Bake 45 to 55 minutes or until a toothpick inserted in center of cake comes out clean. Cool in pan 10 minutes; turn onto a wire rack to cool completely.

For glaze, combine jam and nectar in a small saucepan over medium heat; stir until well blended. Pour evenly over top of cake. Store in an airtight container.
Yield: about 20 servings

CHOCOLATE-NUT COFFEE CAKE

- 1/2 cup firmly packed brown sugar
- 1/2 cup semisweet chocolate mini chips
- 1/2 cup finely chopped walnuts
- 1 tablespoon ground cinnamon
- 3/4 cup butter or margarine, softened
- 1 1/2 cups granulated sugar
- 3 eggs
- 1 tablespoon instant coffee granules dissolved in 1 tablespoon hot water
- 2 teaspoons vanilla extract
- 3 cups all-purpose flour
- 1 1/2 teaspoons baking powder
- 1 1/2 teaspoons baking soda
- 1/4 teaspoon salt
- 1 1/2 cups sour cream

Preheat oven to 350 degrees. In a medium bowl, combine brown sugar, chocolate chips, walnuts, and cinnamon; set aside. In a large bowl, cream butter and sugar until fluffy. Add eggs, 1 at a time, beating well after each addition. Add coffee and vanilla; beat until well blended. In a medium bowl, combine flour, baking powder, baking soda, and salt. Alternately stir dry ingredients and sour cream into creamed mixture, stirring just until well blended. Spoon one-third of batter into bottom of a greased and floured 10-inch tube pan with a removable bottom. Spoon one-third of chocolate chip mixture over batter. Repeat layers, ending with chocolate chip mixture. Bake 1 hour or until a toothpick inserted in center of cake comes out clean. Cool cake in pan on a wire rack 10 minutes. Run a knife around edge of pan; remove sides of pan. Allow cake to cool completely. Run knife around bottom of cake and remove bottom of pan. Store in an airtight container.
Yield: about 16 servings

PUMPKIN-WALNUT PIES

CRUST
- 2 1/4 cups all-purpose flour
- 1/2 teaspoon salt
- 1/2 cup vegetable shortening, chilled
- 1/4 cup chilled butter or margarine
- 1/4 cup ice water

FILLING
- 3/4 cup canned pumpkin
- 1/3 cup granulated sugar
- 1/4 cup firmly packed brown sugar
- 2 eggs
- 1/4 cup dark corn syrup
- 1/2 teaspoon vanilla extract
- 2 teaspoons all-purpose flour
- 3/4 teaspoon pumpkin pie spice
- 1/4 cup evaporated milk
- 3/4 cup finely chopped walnuts

For crust, combine flour and salt in a medium bowl. Using a pastry blender or 2 knives, cut in shortening and butter until mixture resembles coarse meal. Sprinkle with water; mix until a soft dough forms. Shape dough into a ball. Wrap with plastic wrap and chill.

Preheat oven to 350 degrees. For filling, beat pumpkin, sugars, eggs, corn syrup, and vanilla in a medium bowl until well blended. In a small bowl, combine flour and pumpkin pie spice. Add dry ingredients and evaporated milk to pumpkin mixture; beat until well blended. Stir in walnuts. Shape dough into 1-inch balls; press 1 ball into bottom and up sides of each cup of an ungreased miniature muffin pan. Place 1 tablespoon pumpkin mixture in each crust. Bake 15 to 20 minutes or until center is almost set. Cool pies in pan on a wire rack 5 minutes. Serve warm or transfer to wire rack to cool completely. Store in an airtight container in refrigerator.
Yield: about 3 dozen mini pies

PRALINE COFFEE

- 1 1/2 quarts strongly brewed coffee
- 2 cans (12 ounces each) evaporated milk
- 1 1/2 cups firmly packed brown sugar
- 1 1/2 cups pecan-flavored liqueur

In a Dutch oven, combine coffee, evaporated milk, and brown sugar. Stirring occasionally, cook over medium-high heat until sugar dissolves and mixture is heated through; remove from heat. Stir in liqueur. Serve hot.
Yield: about fourteen 6-ounce servings

Warm your guests with our creamy homemade Praline Coffee laced with liqueur. To accompany this delicious drink, we suggest Chocolate-Nut Coffee Cake (top left), which is layered and crowned with a sweet, nutty mixture spiced with cinnamon. Bite-size Pumpkin-Walnut Pies (bottom right) are yummy morsels, too!

CRANBERRY-APPLE STRUDEL

5 cups peeled, cored, and very thinly sliced baking apples (about 2 pounds)
2 cups granulated sugar
1¼ cups fresh cranberries
¼ cup apple juice
2 tablespoons cornstarch
2 teaspoons grated lemon zest
¾ teaspoon ground cinnamon
¼ teaspoon ground allspice
⅛ teaspoon salt
1 package (16 ounces) frozen phyllo dough, thawed
½ cup butter or margarine, melted and divided
Confectioners sugar

Preheat oven to 375 degrees. For filling, combine apple slices, granulated sugar, cranberries, apple juice, cornstarch, lemon zest, cinnamon, allspice, and salt in a large saucepan over medium-high heat; stir constantly until mixture begins to boil. Reduce heat to medium and continue stirring until mixture thickens. Remove from heat and cool to room temperature.

To assemble strudel, place a large damp cloth (about 14 x 36 inches) on a flat surface. Working quickly, place short sides of 2 sheets of phyllo dough along one short side of cloth. Overlapping short edges 2 inches, place next 2 sheets of dough on towel. Brush dough with melted butter. Continue layering dough and brushing with butter, reserving 1 tablespoon butter. Beginning 4 inches from one short edge of dough, spread filling to cover an area about 5 inches wide and 12 inches long (**Fig. 1**).

Fig. 1

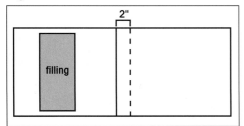

Cranberry-Apple Strudel, a favorite German treat, features flaky pastry with a tart cranberry and apple filling tucked inside. Brushed with melted butter and baked until golden brown, the strudel has a sprinkling of confectioners sugar. Honey adds sweetness to full-bodied Honey-Rum Coffee.

Beginning at filled edge of dough, hold short edge of cloth and pull dough over filling. Continue to fold dough and filling. Using cloth, transfer strudel, seam side down, to a greased 10½ by 15½-inch jellyroll pan. Make cuts with a knife across strudel at about 1-inch intervals. Brush top of strudel with reserved butter. Bake 30 to 40 minutes or until golden brown. Place pan on a wire rack. Sift confectioners sugar over warm strudel. Slice strudel at cuts; serve warm or cool completely.
Yield: about 12 servings

HONEY-RUM COFFEE

1 can (12 ounces) evaporated milk
6 tablespoons honey
1½ quarts strongly brewed hot coffee
½ cup dark rum

In a Dutch oven, combine evaporated milk and honey. Stirring occasionally, cook over medium-high heat until milk is warm. Add coffee; stir until well blended. Remove from heat. Stir in rum. Serve hot.
Yield: about ten 6-ounce servings

APRICOT WINE CORDIAL

- 12 ounces dried apricots
- 1 bottle (1.5 liters) dry white wine
- 2 cups sugar
- 1 cup apricot-flavored brandy

Process apricots in a food processor until finely chopped. Place apricots in a nonmetal container. Stir in wine, sugar, and brandy. Cover and allow to stand at room temperature 1 to 4 weeks. Strain wine and pour into gift bottles. Reserve fruit for Lemon Cakes with Apricot Sauce.

Yield: about 7 cups wine

LEMON CAKES WITH APRICOT SAUCE

CAKE

- 1 cup butter or margarine, softened
- 1 cup sugar
- 4 eggs
- 3/4 cup sour cream
- 1/4 cup fresh lemon juice
- 1 tablespoon grated lemon zest
- 1 teaspoon vanilla extract
- 2 1/4 cups cake flour
- 1 teaspoon baking powder
- 1/4 teaspoon salt

SAUCE

- 1 cup water
- 3/4 cup sugar
- 3 cups reserved fruit from Apricot Wine Cordial **or** combine 12 ounces finely chopped dried apricots and 1/2 cup apricot brandy

Preheat oven to 350 degrees. For cake, cream butter and sugar in a large bowl until fluffy. Add eggs, 1 at a time, beating well after each addition. Add sour cream, lemon juice, lemon zest, and vanilla; beat until well blended. In a medium bowl, combine dry ingredients; add to creamed mixture, stirring until smooth. Spoon about 1/4 cup batter into each cup of a greased shortcake pan. Bake 17 to 19 minutes or until a toothpick inserted in center of cake comes out clean. Cool

For flavorful Apricot Wine Cordial, chopped apricots are marinated in sweetened white wine and brandy for several weeks. Scrumptious little Lemon Cakes are served with candied Apricot Sauce made from the reserved fruit pieces. Baked in shortcake pans, the cakes are just right for individual servings.

in pan 5 minutes. Turn cakes onto a wire rack to cool completely.

For sauce, combine water and sugar in a medium saucepan over medium-high heat. Cook until sugar dissolves and mixture comes to a boil. Reduce heat to medium; cover and cook 2 minutes. Remove from heat; cool 20 minutes. Stir fruit into sugar syrup. Spoon sauce over individual cakes to serve.

Yield: about 18 cakes

Dressed up with raspberry sauce and plump whole berries, Raspberry-Cream Cheese Brownie Pie is a fudgy delight. It begins with a brownie layer that's covered with a rich chocolate-cream cheese mixture.

RASPBERRY-CREAM CHEESE BROWNIE PIE

1   package (10 ounces) raspberry-
    flavored semisweet chocolate
    chips, divided
1   cup butter or margarine, softened
2   cups sugar, divided
3   eggs
2   teaspoons vanilla extract, divided
2   cups all-purpose flour
1/2   teaspoon baking powder
11   ounces (one 8-ounce package
    and one 3-ounce package)
    cream cheese, softened
1   egg
1   jar (12 ounces) seedless
    raspberry jam
    Frozen red raspberries to garnish

Preheat oven to 350 degrees. In a small microwave-safe bowl, microwave 1 cup chocolate chips on medium-high power (80%) 2 minutes or until chocolate softens; stir until smooth. In a large bowl, beat butter and 1 2/3 cups sugar until fluffy. Add 3 eggs, 1 at a time, beating well after each addition. Stir in melted chocolate and 1 teaspoon vanilla. In a small bowl, combine flour and baking powder. Add dry ingredients to creamed mixture; stir until well blended. Line a 9-inch springform pan with aluminum foil; grease foil. Spread chocolate mixture into prepared pan. Bake 40 minutes.

In a small microwave-safe bowl, microwave remaining 2/3 cup chocolate chips on medium-high power (80%) 2 minutes or until chocolate softens; stir until smooth. In a large bowl, beat cream cheese and remaining 1/3 cup sugar until smooth. Add 1 egg and remaining 1 teaspoon vanilla; beat until smooth. Stir in melted chocolate. Gently spread cream cheese mixture over warm brownie layer. Bake 15 minutes or until cream cheese mixture is set. Cool in pan on a wire rack. Cover and chill.

To serve, melt raspberry jam in a heavy small saucepan over medium heat. Remove from heat; cool 10 minutes. Remove sides of springform pan. Spoon melted raspberry jam over each piece of brownie pie. Garnish with frozen raspberries.
Yield: about 16 servings

An attractive arrangement of pecan halves accents our Chocolate-Pecan Tart, which is loaded with chocolate chips and pecans baked in a sweet filling.

CHOCOLATE-PECAN TART

CRUST
1 1/4 cups all-purpose flour
2 tablespoons sugar
1/4 teaspoon ground cinnamon
1/4 cup butter or margarine, softened
1/4 cup vegetable shortening
1 egg yolk
1/2 teaspoon vanilla extract

FILLING
1/2 cup semisweet chocolate mini chips
1 1/4 cups pecan halves
3 tablespoons granulated sugar
3 tablespoons firmly packed brown sugar
1/8 teaspoon salt
3 tablespoons butter or margarine, melted
1/2 cup dark corn syrup
3 eggs
1 teaspoon vanilla extract

For crust, combine flour, sugar, and cinnamon in a medium bowl. Using a pastry blender or 2 knives, cut in butter and shortening until mixture resembles coarse meal. Add egg yolk and vanilla; mix just until blended. Firmly press pastry into bottom and up sides of a 9-inch-diameter tart pan with a removable bottom. Chill 30 minutes.

Preheat oven to 400 degrees. Prick bottom of tart shell with a fork. Bake 5 minutes. Allow to cool 15 minutes.

For filling, reduce oven temperature to 350 degrees. Sprinkle chocolate chips over cooled crust. Arrange pecan halves on chocolate chips. In a medium bowl, combine sugars and salt. Stir in melted butter and corn syrup. Add eggs and vanilla; whisk until well blended. Slowly pour mixture over pecans in crust. Bake 40 to 45 minutes or until filling is almost set. Place tart on a wire rack to cool. Remove sides of pan to serve.
Yield: about 10 servings

CHOCOLATE CREAM PIE

CRUST
1 1/2 cups all-purpose flour
1/2 teaspoon salt
1/2 cup vegetable shortening
3 to 4 tablespoons cold water

FILLING
1 cup sugar
1/4 cup cocoa
1/4 cup cornstarch
1 3/4 cups milk
3 tablespoons butter or margarine
3 egg yolks, beaten
2 tablespoons orange-flavored liqueur
1 teaspoon vanilla extract

MERINGUE
4 egg whites
1/2 teaspoon cream of tartar
1 teaspoon orange-flavored liqueur
1/2 cup sifted confectioners sugar

For crust, combine flour and salt in a medium bowl. Using a pastry blender or 2 knives, cut in shortening until mixture resembles coarse meal. Sprinkle with water; mix until a soft dough forms. On a lightly floured surface, use a floured rolling pin to roll out dough to 1/8-inch thickness. Transfer to a 9-inch pie plate and use a sharp knife to trim edge of dough. Prick bottom of crust with a fork. Chill 30 minutes.

Preheat oven to 450 degrees. Bake crust 10 to 12 minutes or until lightly browned. Cool completely on a wire rack.

For filling, combine sugar, cocoa, and cornstarch in a heavy medium saucepan. Stir in milk and butter. Stirring constantly, cook over medium heat until mixture thickens and begins to boil. Continuing to stir, boil 1 minute. Remove from heat. Add about 1/2 cup chocolate mixture to egg yolks; stir until well blended. Gradually add egg mixture to chocolate mixture in saucepan, stirring until well blended. Return to medium heat and bring to a boil; boil 1 minute or until mixture coats the back of a spoon. Stir in liqueur and vanilla. Remove filling from heat; pour into crust.

Preheat oven to 350 degrees. For meringue, beat egg whites and cream of tartar in a medium bowl until foamy. Add liqueur. Gradually add confectioners sugar, beating until stiff peaks form. Spread meringue over filling. Bake 10 to 15 minutes or until golden brown. Serve warm or chilled. Store in an airtight container in refrigerator.

Yield: about 10 servings

ORANGE MARMALADE CAKE

CAKE
3/4 cup butter or margarine, softened
1 cup sugar
3 eggs
1 teaspoon vanilla extract
3/4 cup orange marmalade
2 1/2 cups all-purpose flour
1 teaspoon baking soda
1/2 cup buttermilk

ICING
1 cup sugar
1/3 cup milk
1 can (15 1/2 ounces) crushed pineapple, drained
1/2 cup flaked coconut
1/2 cup finely chopped pecans, toasted
2 tablespoons orange marmalade

Preheat oven to 350 degrees. For cake, cream butter and sugar in a large bowl until fluffy. Add eggs and vanilla; beat until smooth. Stir in marmalade. Sift flour and baking soda into a medium bowl. Alternately beat dry ingredients and buttermilk into creamed mixture. Pour batter into a greased and floured 8 1/2-inch fluted tube pan. Bake 40 to 45 minutes or until a toothpick inserted in center of cake comes out clean. Cool in pan on a wire rack 10 minutes; invert onto a serving plate.

For icing, combine sugar and milk in a heavy medium saucepan. Stirring constantly, cook over medium-low heat until sugar dissolves. Using a pastry brush dipped in hot water, wash down any sugar crystals on sides of pan. Attach a candy thermometer to pan, making sure thermometer does not touch bottom of pan. Bring to a boil. Cook, without stirring, until syrup reaches 230 degrees. Remove from heat; pour into a heat-resistant bowl. Using medium speed of an electric mixer, beat mixture until thickened and creamy. Stir in pineapple, coconut, pecans, and marmalade. Spoon over cake. Store in an airtight container in refrigerator.

Yield: about 16 servings

Generously crowned with a nutty blend of coconut and fruit, Orange Marmalade Cake (left) is a moist, tangy dessert. Fluffy meringue tops a chocolaty filling for our Chocolate Cream Pie (top right).

BLACK FOREST CHEESECAKE

Cheesecake must be made 1 day in advance.

CHOCOLATE DECORATIONS
$^1/_2$ cup semisweet chocolate chips

CRUST
1 package (12 ounces) vanilla wafer cookies, finely crushed
$^3/_4$ cup butter or margarine, melted

FILLING
1 package (12 ounces) semisweet chocolate chips, divided
20 ounces cream cheese, softened
$^3/_4$ cup sugar
3 eggs
1 egg yolk
2 tablespoons whipping cream
1 tablespoon vanilla extract
2 teaspoons all-purpose flour

TOPPING
2 cans (16 ounces each) tart red pitted cherries
$^1/_4$ cup cornstarch
1 cup sugar

DECORATIVE TOPPING
2 tablespoons water
$1^1/_2$ teaspoons unflavored gelatin
2 tablespoons sugar
$^1/_2$ cup whipping cream
Maraschino cherries with stems

For chocolate decorations, melt chocolate chips in a small saucepan over low heat, stirring constantly. Spoon chocolate into a pastry bag fitted with a small round tip. For each decoration, pipe chocolate onto waxed paper, forming a $2^1/_2$-inch-high triangle. Randomly pipe chocolate inside triangle, making sure piped lines overlap. Repeat to make 16 decorations. Allow chocolate to harden. Store in a cool, dry place until ready to decorate cake.

For crust, combine cookie crumbs and butter. Press into bottom and halfway up sides of a greased 9-inch springform pan. Cover and refrigerate.

For filling, melt 1 cup chocolate chips in a small saucepan over low heat, stirring constantly; remove from heat. Adding 1 package at a time, beat cream cheese 25 minutes in a large bowl. Preheat oven to 500 degrees. Add sugar and melted chocolate to cream cheese; beat 5 minutes longer. Add eggs and egg yolk, 1 at a time, beating 2 minutes after each addition. Beat in whipping cream, vanilla, and flour. Stir in remaining 1 cup chocolate chips. Pour filling into crust. Bake 10 minutes. Reduce heat to 200 degrees. Bake 1 hour. Turn oven off and leave cake in oven 1 hour without opening door. Cool completely on a wire rack. Remove sides of pan.

For topping, drain cherries, reserving $^1/_4$ cup juice. In a small bowl, combine cornstarch and reserved cherry juice. In a medium saucepan, combine cherries and sugar. Stirring occasionally, cook over medium heat until sugar dissolves and mixture comes to a boil. Stirring constantly, add cornstarch mixture and cook until thickened. Remove from heat; cool to room temperature. Spoon cherry mixture over cheesecake. Store in an airtight container 8 hours or overnight in refrigerator.

For decorative topping, place a large bowl and beaters from an electric mixer in freezer until well chilled. In a small saucepan, combine water and gelatin; let stand 1 minute. Stir in sugar; cook over low heat, stirring until gelatin and sugar dissolve. Remove from heat. In chilled bowl, beat whipping cream until soft peaks form. Add sugar mixture and beat until stiff peaks form. Spoon whipped cream mixture into a pastry bag fitted with a large star tip; pipe mixture onto cake. Carefully peel waxed paper from chocolate decorations. Place chocolate decorations and cherries on cake. Store in an airtight container in refrigerator.
Yield: 16 servings

RASPBERRY ANGEL FOOD CAKE

CAKE
1 package (12 ounces) frozen raspberries, thawed
1 purchased angel food cake (9-inch diameter)

FROSTING
1 package (8 ounces) cream cheese, softened
2 cups sifted confectioners sugar
2 tablespoons sour cream
2 tablespoons crème de cassis liqueur
Red food coloring
Fresh red raspberries to garnish

Drain thawed raspberries, reserving juice. Cut cake in half horizontally; remove top layer. Spoon raspberries evenly over bottom layer of cake. Reserving 2 tablespoons juice for frosting, pour remaining juice evenly over raspberries on cake. Replace top layer of cake.

For frosting, beat cream cheese until fluffy using medium speed of an electric mixer. Add reserved juice and confectioners sugar, sour cream, and liqueur; stir until well blended. Tint with food coloring. Transfer $^1/_2$ cup frosting to a pastry bag fitted with a large star tip. Spread remaining frosting on sides and top of cake. Pipe a decorative border along bottom and top edges of cake. Garnish with fresh raspberries. Store in an airtight container in refrigerator.
Yield: about 16 servings

A wonderful variation of a favorite dessert, Black Forest Cheesecake (top) is a luscious chocolate cheesecake with a sweet cherry topping. Each slice has a garnish of whipped cream, a cherry, and a delicate chocolate lattice. Elegant, easy-to-make Raspberry Angel Food Cake (bottom) is heaven-sent. This delicate cake features a creamy frosting and lots of fresh berries.

FUDGE-TOPPED PUMPKIN PIE

- 1   9-inch frozen pumpkin pie (about 40 ounces)
- 1¼ cups semisweet chocolate chips
- 2   tablespoons honey
- 2   teaspoons vegetable shortening
- ¼ teaspoon orange extract
- 1   cup chopped pecans, toasted
  Pecan halves to garnish

Bake pumpkin pie according to package directions. Remove from oven and place on a wire rack. Place chocolate chips in a small microwave-safe bowl. Microwave on medium-high power (80%) 1 minute; stir. Continue to microwave 15 seconds at a time, stirring until smooth. Add honey, shortening, and orange extract; stir until well blended. Stir in chopped pecans. Spread topping over hot pie. Allow pie to cool 1 hour. Garnish with pecan halves and serve warm.
Yield: about 10 servings

APRICOT-NUT FRUITCAKE

Make at least 1 day in advance.

CAKE

- 1   package (18¼ ounces) yellow cake mix
- 1   package (8 ounces) cream cheese, softened
- 1   package (3½ ounces) vanilla pudding mix
- 4   eggs
- ⅓ cup vegetable oil
- ¼ cup water
- ¼ cup apricot brandy
- 1   package (6 ounces) dried apricots, coarsely chopped
- 2   cups coarsely chopped pecans

GLAZE

- ¼ cup apricot preserves
- ¼ cup apricot brandy

Preheat oven to 350 degrees. For cake, combine cake mix, cream cheese, pudding mix, eggs, oil, water, and brandy in a large bowl. Beat at low speed of an electric mixer until

Our Apricot-Nut Fruitcake (left), made with packaged cake and pudding mixes, will give you a head start on your big event. Preparing the cake a day in advance allows the spirited glaze to reach peak flavor. Fudge-Topped Pumpkin Pie begins with a purchased frozen pie that you improve with a chocolaty homemade glaze. Served warm, it's simply delicious!

moistened. Beat at medium speed 2 minutes longer. Stir in apricots and pecans. Pour into a greased and floured 10-inch fluted tube pan. Bake 55 to 60 minutes or until a toothpick inserted in center of cake comes out clean. Allow cake to cool in pan 10 minutes. Invert onto a serving plate.

For glaze, combine preserves and brandy in a small bowl; spoon over warm cake. Cool cake completely. Cover and allow to stand at room temperature 24 hours before serving.
Yield: about 16 servings

Pumpkin Cheesecake Squares are sure to be enjoyed! For this luscious dessert, pumpkin and spice cheesecake is sandwiched between a nutty graham cracker crust and rich praline topping.

PUMPKIN CHEESECAKE SQUARES

CRUST
- 1 cup graham cracker crumbs
- 1/2 cup chopped walnuts, finely ground
- 1/4 cup sugar
- 1/2 teaspoon pumpkin pie spice
- 1/4 teaspoon ground cinnamon
- 1/4 teaspoon ground nutmeg
- 1/4 cup butter or margarine, melted

FILLING
- 12 ounces cream cheese, softened
- 3/4 cup firmly packed brown sugar
- 3 eggs
- 3/4 cup canned pumpkin
- 1/2 teaspoon orange extract
- 1/2 teaspoon ground cinnamon
- 1/2 teaspoon pumpkin pie spice
- 1/4 teaspoon ground nutmeg

TOPPING
- 1 cup butter or margarine
- 1 cup firmly packed brown sugar
- 1/2 teaspoon pumpkin pie spice
- 1 1/2 cups chopped walnuts

Preheat oven to 350 degrees. For crust, combine cracker crumbs, walnuts, sugar, pumpkin pie spice, cinnamon, and nutmeg in a large bowl. Add butter; stir until mixture is crumbly. Press into bottom of a greased 9 x 13-inch glass baking dish; set aside.

For filling, beat cream cheese and brown sugar in a large bowl until fluffy. Add eggs, pumpkin, orange extract, cinnamon, pumpkin pie spice, and nutmeg; beat until well blended. Pour over crust. Bake 55 to 60 minutes or until set in center. Cool completely on a wire rack.

For topping, combine butter, brown sugar, and pumpkin pie spice in a medium saucepan. Stirring constantly, cook over medium heat until sugar dissolves. Bring to a boil and cook 2 to 3 minutes or until syrup thickens. Stir in walnuts. Pour over cooled filling. Cool completely. Cover and refrigerate until ready to serve. Cut into squares to serve. Store in refrigerator.

Yield: about 2 dozen squares

Delightfully rich and sweet, Orange Black Bottom Pie features a layer of chocolate topped with a creamy orange filling. Sweetened whipped cream is piped around the edge for an elegant finish.

ORANGE BLACK BOTTOM PIE

CRUST
1 1/2 cups all-purpose flour
 1/2 teaspoon salt
 1/2 cup vegetable shortening
 3 to 4 tablespoons cold water

FILLING
 3/4 cup whipping cream, divided
 1/2 cup semisweet chocolate chips
 2 tablespoons butter or margarine
 2 teaspoons orange extract, divided
 1 cup water
 1 package (3 ounces) orange gelatin
 1 package (8 ounces) cream cheese, softened
 1 cup sifted confectioners sugar

DECORATIVE TOPPING
 2 tablespoons water
 2 tablespoons sugar
1 1/2 teaspoons unflavored gelatin
 1/2 cup whipping cream

For crust, preheat oven to 450 degrees. Sift flour and salt into a medium bowl. Using a pastry blender or 2 knives, cut in shortening until mixture resembles coarse meal. Sprinkle with water; mix until a soft dough forms. On a lightly floured surface, use a floured rolling pin to roll out dough to 1/8-inch thickness. Cut out a 13-inch-diameter circle. Press dough into bottom and up sides of a 9-inch deep-dish pie plate; trim edges of dough. Prick bottom of crust with a fork. Bake 12 to 15 minutes or until light brown. Cool completely.

For filling, combine 1/4 cup whipping cream, chocolate chips, and butter in a small saucepan. Stirring constantly, cook over low heat until smooth. Stir in 1 teaspoon orange extract. Pour into cooled crust.

Chill medium bowl and beaters from an electric mixer in freezer. In a medium saucepan, bring water to a boil. Add orange gelatin; stir until dissolved. Remove from heat; cool to room temperature.

In a large bowl, beat cream cheese, confectioners sugar, and remaining 1 teaspoon orange extract until fluffy. Beat gelatin mixture into cream cheese mixture. In chilled bowl, whip remaining 1/2 cup whipping cream until stiff peaks form. Fold whipped cream into cream cheese mixture. Return bowl and beaters to freezer. Pour filling evenly over chocolate mixture. Cover and refrigerate until pie is set.

For decorative topping, combine water, sugar, and gelatin in a small saucepan; let stand 1 minute. Stirring constantly, cook over low heat until gelatin and sugar dissolve. Remove from heat. In chilled bowl, beat whipping cream until soft peaks form. Add sugar mixture and beat until stiff peaks form. Transfer topping to a pastry bag fitted with a large star tip. Pipe a decorative border along top edge of pie. Cover and refrigerate until ready to serve.

Yield: about 8 servings

PEAR-GINGER PIE

CRUST

- 2 cups all-purpose flour
- 1 teaspoon salt
- 2/3 cup vegetable shortening
- 7 to 9 tablespoons cold water

FILLING

- 1 bottle (2 ounces) crystallized ginger, minced
- 3 pounds ripe pears (about 7 pears), peeled, cored, and coarsely chopped
- 3/4 cup sugar
- 2 tablespoons quick-cooking tapioca
- 1 tablespoon lemon juice
- 1 1/4 teaspoons ground cinnamon
- 1/4 teaspoon ground nutmeg
- 3/4 cup chopped walnuts

GLAZE

- 1 egg
- 1 tablespoon milk

For crust, sift flour and salt into a medium bowl. Using a pastry blender or 2 knives, cut in shortening until mixture resembles coarse meal. Sprinkle with water; mix until a soft dough forms. Divide dough into 2 balls. On a lightly floured surface, use a floured rolling pin to roll out 1 ball of dough to 1/8-inch thickness. Transfer to an ungreased 9-inch deep-dish pie plate and use a sharp knife to trim edges of dough. Roll out remaining dough to 1/8-inch thickness. Use a sharp knife to cut an 11-inch-diameter circle. Using a 1-inch star-shaped cookie cutter, cut 4 stars from dough scraps. Cover all dough; set aside.

Preheat oven to 400 degrees. For filling, place ginger in a small saucepan and add enough water to cover. Bring water to a boil; reduce heat to low. Stirring occasionally, simmer about 15 minutes or until all water is absorbed. Remove from heat; set aside.

In a large bowl, combine pears, sugar, tapioca, lemon juice, cinnamon,

Chopped walnuts add distinctive flavor to spicy Pear-Ginger Pie. For a festive look, the top crust is garnished with star cutouts.

nutmeg, and walnuts. Add ginger mixture to pear mixture; stir until well blended. Spoon pear mixture evenly into crust. Place top crust over filling. Fold edge of top crust under edge of bottom crust. Pinch edges together to seal.

For glaze, combine egg and milk in a small bowl. Brush egg mixture evenly over crust. Place stars on crust. Brush egg mixture on stars. Cut slits in top of pie. Bake 50 to 55 minutes or until crust is golden brown. Serve warm or at room temperature.

Yield: about 8 servings

GIFTS OF GOOD TASTE

*H*omemade goodies prepared in your own kitchen for friends and loved ones are gifts from the heart! The thoughtfulness and personal touches that go hand in hand with these treats only add to their appeal. In this section, you'll find an abundant sampling of Yuletide delights that taste great and promise to please the very special people on your gift list. From sauces and spreads to snacks and sweets, these yummy offerings will pass along the joy of this festive season to the people you hold dear.

Sweet, zesty Roasted Red Pepper Jelly (recipe on page 140) is a versatile condiment that makes a savory accompaniment to a meat dish. It's also perfect for perking up an appetizer such as cream cheese and crackers.

No-bake Chocolate-Nut Truffles are easy to prepare with rich chocolate-flavored liqueur, vanilla wafer crumbs, and toasted pecans. Rolled in confectioners sugar, the yummy treats are melt-in-your-mouth good!

ROASTED RED PEPPER JELLY (Shown on page 139)

- 6 large sweet red peppers
- 6 cups sugar
- 1 cup white wine vinegar
- 2 pouches (3 ounces each) liquid fruit pectin

To roast peppers, cut in half lengthwise and remove seeds and membranes. Place, skin side up, on an ungreased baking sheet; flatten with hand. Broil about 3 inches from heat about 15 to 20 minutes or until peppers are blackened and charred. Immediately seal peppers in a plastic bag and allow to steam 10 to 15 minutes. Remove charred skin. In a food processor, process peppers until finely chopped. In a heavy large saucepan, combine peppers, sugar, and vinegar until well blended. Stirring constantly over high heat, bring pepper mixture to a rolling boil. Stir in liquid pectin. Stirring constantly, bring to a rolling boil again and boil 1 minute. Remove from heat; skim off foam. Spoon jelly into heat-resistant jars; cover and cool to room temperature. Store in refrigerator.

Yield: about 3¹/₂ pints jelly

CHOCOLATE-NUT TRUFFLES

- 2 cups vanilla wafer crumbs
- 2 cups sifted confectioners sugar
- 1 cup finely chopped pecans, toasted
- 2 tablespoons cocoa
- 4¹/₂ tablespoons whipping cream
- 4¹/₂ tablespoons chocolate-flavored liqueur
  Sifted confectioners sugar

In a large bowl, combine vanilla wafer crumbs, 2 cups confectioners sugar, pecans, and cocoa. Add whipping cream and liqueur; stir until well blended. Shape into 1-inch balls; roll in confectioners sugar. Store in an airtight container in a cool place.

Yield: about 5 dozen candies

CHICKEN PIES

FILLING

 1 cup frozen hash brown potatoes
 1 cup (about ½ pound) finely chopped uncooked chicken
 1 large onion, finely chopped
 ¼ cup shredded carrot
 ¼ cup finely chopped turnip
 2 teaspoons garlic powder
 ½ teaspoon salt
 ½ teaspoon ground black pepper

PASTRY

 4 cups all-purpose flour
 2 teaspoons salt
 1 cup butter-flavored shortening
 1 cup ice water
 ½ cup butter or margarine, melted

For filling, combine potatoes, chicken, onion, carrot, turnip, garlic powder, salt, and pepper in a large bowl; stir until well blended. Cover and refrigerate until ready to use.

Preheat oven to 375 degrees. For pastry, sift flour and salt into a large bowl. Using a pastry blender or 2 knives, cut shortening into flour mixture until mixture resembles coarse meal. Slowly add water, mixing until a soft dough forms. Turn dough onto a lightly floured surface and use a floured rolling pin to roll out dough to ¼-inch thickness. Use a 3-inch heart-shaped cookie cutter to cut out an even number of heart shapes. Transfer half of heart shapes to a greased baking sheet; spoon about 2 tablespoons filling in center of each heart shape. Place remaining heart shapes over filling. To seal, crimp edges with a fork. Brush tops with melted butter. Bake 45 to 50 minutes or until golden brown. Transfer to a wire rack to cool completely. Store in an airtight container in refrigerator. Give with serving instructions.

Yield: about 1½ dozen pies
To serve: Preheat oven to 350 degrees. Bake uncovered 10 to 15 minutes or until heated through.

A basket of Chicken Pies is a tasty way to express your heartfelt appreciation to a friend. The flaky little pies are cut into heart shapes and filled with tender chicken and vegetables.

CHRISTMAS PRETZELS

Vanilla candy coating
Green and red powdered food
coloring **or** oil-based candy
coloring
1 package (10 ounces) large
Bavarian-style pretzels
1 package (10 ounces) small
pretzel twists
White candy nonpareils

Stirring constantly, melt desired amount of candy coating in a small saucepan over low heat; tint green or red. Using a fork, dip one pretzel at a time into coating, covering completely. Transfer to a wire rack with waxed paper underneath. Before coating hardens, sprinkle pretzels with nonpareils. Allow coating to harden. Store in an airtight container in a cool place.
Yield: about 12 cups coated pretzels

MARINATED FRUIT MEDLEY

5 small oranges, peeled, seeded, and sliced
2 kiwi fruit, peeled and sliced
1 jar (6 ounces) maraschino cherries, drained
1 cup orange-flavored liqueur
1 teaspoon anise seed
1/2 cup sugar

Combine oranges, kiwi fruit, cherries, liqueur, anise seed, and sugar in a large bowl. Stir until sugar dissolves. Cover and chill 8 hours or overnight to allow flavors to blend.

Serve alone or with ice cream or shortcake. Store in an airtight container in refrigerator.
Yield: about 3 cups fruit

Dipped in red- and green-tinted candy coating, Christmas Pretzels are a dressed-up version of a popular snack. The festive pretzels also make wonderful edible ornaments for a tabletop tree.

PEANUT BUTTER SNACK MIX

- 2 bags (11 ounces each) small pretzels
- 1 package (12 ounces) peanut butter chips
- 1 jar (7 ounces) marshmallow creme
- 1/2 cup butter or margarine
- 1/4 cup honey
- 1/4 cup milk
- 6 cups confectioners sugar

Place pretzels in a very large bowl. Stirring constantly, melt peanut butter chips in a medium saucepan over low heat. Add marshmallow creme, butter, honey, and milk; stir until smooth. Pour peanut butter mixture over pretzels; stir until evenly coated. Place 2 cups confectioners sugar into a large plastic bag. Add one-third of pretzel mixture; close bag and shake briefly. Spread mix on waxed paper. Repeat with remaining confectioners sugar and pretzels. Cool completely. Store in an airtight container.

Yield: about 23 cups snack mix

Make yummy Peanut Butter Snack Mix by covering pretzels with honey-sweetened marshmallow creme and peanut butter chips, then coating with confectioners sugar.

Oranges, kiwi fruit, and cherries make a colorful showing in this Marinated Fruit Medley. Great for spooning over ice cream or cake, the mixture gets its deliciously different taste from orange liqueur and anise seed.

CHERRY-ALMOND CHRISTMAS WREATH

BREAD
- 1 package dry yeast
- 1/4 cup warm water
- 1/2 cup butter or margarine, softened
- 1/4 cup warm milk
- 2 tablespoons sugar
- 1 teaspoon ground cardamom
- 1/2 teaspoon salt
- 3 to 3 1/2 cups all-purpose flour, divided
- 2 eggs
  Vegetable cooking spray

FILLING
- 1/2 cup sugar
- 1/2 cup almond paste
- 1/3 cup butter or margarine, softened
- 1 teaspoon almond extract
- 3/4 cup red and green candied cherries, divided
- 1/2 cup sliced almonds, toasted

ICING
- 1 cup sifted confectioners sugar
- 2 tablespoons milk
- 1/4 teaspoon almond extract

For bread, dissolve yeast in warm water in a large bowl. Stir in butter, milk, sugar, cardamom, salt, and 1 cup flour. Stir in eggs and enough remaining flour to form a soft dough. Turn onto a lightly floured surface and knead 5 minutes or until dough becomes smooth and elastic. Place in a large bowl sprayed with cooking spray, turning once to coat top of dough. Cover and let rise in a warm place (80 to 85 degrees) 1 hour or until doubled in size.

For filling, combine sugar, almond paste, butter, and almond extract in a small bowl until well blended. Set aside.

Turn dough onto a lightly floured surface and punch down. Use a floured rolling pin to roll out dough to a 9 x 30-inch rectangle. Spread filling over dough to within 1/2 inch of edges; sprinkle with 1/2 cup cherries and almonds. Beginning at 1 long edge, roll up dough jellyroll style; pinch seam

to seal. Cut dough in half lengthwise; turn cut sides up. Wrap dough halves around each other with cut sides up. Place dough on a greased baking sheet; shape into a wreath and pinch ends together to seal. Place remaining 1/4 cup cherries on top of wreath. Spray with cooking spray. Cover loosely with plastic wrap and let rise in a warm place about 30 minutes or until doubled in size.

Preheat oven to 350 degrees. Bake 30 to 40 minutes or until lightly browned. Transfer to a wire rack to cool completely.

For icing, combine confectioners sugar, milk, and almond extract in a small bowl; stir until smooth. Drizzle icing over bread. Allow icing to harden; wrap in cellophane.

Yield: about 20 servings

A tasty twist on the traditional holiday decoration, our Cherry-Almond Christmas Wreath features candied cherries and crunchy almonds. A buttery almond-flavored filling and a drizzling of sweet icing add richness to this pretty yeast bread.

CANDIED CITRUS PEEL

- 6 navel oranges
- 2 cups sugar
- 1 cup water
- 1 tablespoon light corn syrup
  Sugar
- 1¼ cups semisweet chocolate chips
- 2½ teaspoons vegetable shortening

Peel oranges and cut peel into ¼-inch-wide x 3-inch-long strips. In a large saucepan, combine orange peel and enough water to cover; place over high heat and bring to a boil. Drain peel. Repeat boiling process 2 more times and drain.

In a heavy medium saucepan, combine 2 cups sugar, 1 cup water, and corn syrup. Stirring constantly, cook over medium-low heat until sugar dissolves. Using a pastry brush dipped in hot water, wash down any sugar crystals on sides of pan. Attach a candy thermometer to pan, making sure thermometer does not touch bottom of pan. Increase heat to medium and bring to a boil. Cook, without stirring, until syrup reaches soft-ball stage (approximately 234 to 240 degrees). Test about ½ teaspoon syrup in ice water. Syrup will easily form a ball in ice water but will flatten when held in your hand. Add fruit peel. Stirring often, allow peel to simmer over medium-low heat 30 minutes. Drain peel; if desired, reserve syrup for another use (good as a flavored sweetener). Place peel on a wire rack with waxed paper underneath to dry 15 minutes. Roll peel in sugar to coat. Place pieces of candied peel on wire rack and dry overnight.

In a small heavy saucepan, melt chocolate chips and shortening over low heat. Dip one end of each piece of candied peel into chocolate; place on a baking sheet lined with waxed paper. Chill until chocolate hardens. Store in an airtight container in a cool place.
Yield: about 1¼ pounds candy

Pamper someone special with a gourmet treat! Dipped in chocolate, Candied Citrus Peel has picture-perfect appeal.

BRANDIED NUTS AND HONEY

½ cup **each** unsalted pecan halves, whole unsalted macadamia nuts, whole unsalted hazelnuts, and whole unsalted cashews, toasted
1 cup honey
1 tablespoon brandy extract

Layer nuts in two 8-ounce jars. In a small microwave-safe bowl, combine honey and extract. Microwave on high power (100%) 30 seconds. Pour honey mixture over nuts; screw lids on jars. Serve over ice cream, cake, or muffins.
Yield: about 2 cups nut mixture

BRANDIED SPICE COFFEE

⅓ cup ground coffee
½ teaspoon brandy extract
1½ three-inch-long cinnamon sticks
¼ teaspoon whole cloves
¼ teaspoon whole allspice

Place coffee in a food processor. With processor running, add brandy extract. Stop and scrape sides of container with a spatula. Process 10 seconds longer. Place mix in a resealable plastic bag; add cinnamon sticks, cloves, and allspice. Store in refrigerator. Give with serving instructions.
Yield: mix for eight 6-ounce servings
To serve: Place mix in filter of an automatic drip coffee maker. Add 6 cups water and brew.

A friend who loves to curl up with a good cup of coffee will be delighted with Brandied Spice Coffee. To create this exquisite brew, simply add brandy extract and spices to ordinary ground coffee. Sticks of cinnamon make flavorful stirrers.

A sweet, nutty combo, Brandied Nuts and Honey is excellent atop cake, muffins, or ice cream.

Swirls of icing, slivered almonds, and candied cherries decorate Braided Vanocka Loaf, a Czechoslovakian delicacy. Wooden skewers help the holiday bread keep its intricate shape during baking.

BRAIDED VANOCKA LOAF

BREAD
1 package dry yeast
2/3 cup plus 1 teaspoon sugar, divided
1/4 cup warm water
1 1/4 cups milk
1/2 cup butter or margarine
3/4 teaspoon salt
5 to 5 1/2 cups all-purpose flour, divided
2 eggs
2 teaspoons grated lemon zest
1 teaspoon apple pie spice
1 cup golden raisins

Vegetable cooking spray
3 wooden skewers (4 inches long) to secure braids
1 egg

ICING
1 cup sifted confectioners sugar
2 tablespoons milk
1/4 teaspoon almond extract
Slivered almonds and red and green candied cherry halves to decorate

For bread, dissolve yeast and 1 teaspoon sugar in warm water in a large bowl. In a medium saucepan, combine milk and butter over medium heat, stirring until butter melts; remove from heat. Stir remaining 2/3 cup sugar and salt into milk mixture. Cool mixture to lukewarm. Stir 1 cup flour, 2 eggs, lemon zest, and apple pie spice into yeast mixture. Stir in milk mixture and raisins. Add 4 cups flour; stir until a soft dough forms. Turn dough onto a lightly floured surface. Knead about 5 minutes or until dough becomes smooth and elastic, using additional flour as necessary. Place in a large bowl sprayed with cooking spray, turning once to coat top of dough. Cover and let rise in a warm place (80 to 85 degrees) 1 1/2 hours or until doubled in size.

Turn dough onto a lightly floured surface and punch down. Divide dough into 6 pieces. Cover and allow dough pieces to rest 10 minutes. Roll 3 pieces of dough into 15-inch-long ropes. Place ropes in the center of a lightly greased baking sheet and braid together. Press ends of braid together and tuck under. Lightly roll braid with a rolling pin to flatten. For middle braid, knead 2 pieces of dough together and divide into 3 pieces; roll each into a 12-inch-long rope. Braid ropes together. Lightly brush water on first braid where second braid will be placed. Center second braid on first braid. Press ends of braid together and tuck under. Divide remaining dough into 3 pieces; roll each into an 8-inch-long rope. Braid ropes together. Lightly brush water on second braid where third braid will be placed. Center third braid on second braid. Press ends of braid together and tuck under. To hold braids in place during rising and baking, insert skewers through middle and each end of top braid. Loosely cover dough and let rise at room temperature about 45 minutes or until almost doubled in size.

Preheat oven to 350 degrees. Beat 1 egg in a small bowl. Brush over entire loaf. Bake bread 15 minutes or until lightly browned. Loosely cover with foil and bake 40 minutes or until bread is golden brown and sounds hollow when tapped. Transfer to a wire rack with waxed paper underneath to cool. Remove skewers.

For icing, combine confectioners sugar, milk, and almond extract in a small bowl; stir until smooth. Drizzle icing over bread. Sprinkle almonds over icing and place cherry halves on bread to decorate. Allow icing to harden. Store in an airtight container.
Yield: 1 loaf bread

A batch of our spicy Cherry-Nut Cakes makes a bundle of individually wrapped goodies to share with folks on your gift list. Friends and relatives will clamor for more of these sweet cakes!

CHERRY-NUT CAKES

12 ounces dried cherries (available at gourmet food stores)
1 1/2 cups orange-flavored liqueur
6 tablespoons finely chopped crystallized ginger
1 cup butter or margarine, softened
3/4 cup firmly packed brown sugar
6 eggs
1 tablespoon vanilla extract
1 1/2 cups all-purpose flour
1 teaspoon ground cinnamon
1/2 teaspoon ground nutmeg
1/4 teaspoon ground cloves
2 cups chopped unsalted pecans
2 cups chopped unsalted walnuts
2 cups chopped unsalted cashews

In a small bowl, combine cherries, liqueur, and ginger. Cover and let stand at room temperature 8 hours or overnight.

Preheat oven to 350 degrees. In a large bowl, cream butter and brown sugar until fluffy. Beat in eggs and vanilla. In a small bowl, combine flour, cinnamon, nutmeg, and cloves. Add flour mixture to creamed mixture; stir until smooth. Stir in cherry mixture and nuts. Spoon batter into greased and floured 2 1/2 x 4 1/2-inch loaf pans. Bake 35 to 40 minutes or until a toothpick inserted in center of cake comes out clean. Cool in pans 10 minutes; remove from pans and cool completely on a wire rack. Store in an airtight container.
Yield: about 1 1/2 dozen cakes

MARASCHINO CHERRY BREAD

1 jar (10 ounces) maraschino
cherries
1 cup granulated sugar
2 eggs
1/4 cup vegetable oil
1 teaspoon vanilla extract
1 3/4 cups all-purpose flour
1 1/2 teaspoons baking powder
1/4 teaspoon salt
1 cup chopped pecans
1 cup sifted confectioners sugar

Preheat oven to 350 degrees. Grease two 3 1/2 x 7 1/2-inch loaf pans and line with waxed paper. Drain cherries, reserving juice. Chop cherries; reserve 1 tablespoon for glaze. In a large bowl, combine granulated sugar, eggs, oil, vanilla, chopped cherries, and 1/4 cup reserved cherry juice; beat until well blended. In a small bowl, combine flour, baking powder, and salt. Add dry ingredients to cherry mixture; stir until well blended. Stir in pecans. Spoon batter into prepared pans. Bake 45 to 50 minutes or until a toothpick inserted in center of bread comes out clean and top is golden brown. Cool in pans 10 minutes. Remove from pans and place on a wire rack with waxed paper underneath to cool completely.

Combine confectioners sugar, 2 to 2 1/2 tablespoons reserved cherry juice, and reserved chopped cherries in a small bowl; stir until well blended. Spoon over bread. Allow icing to harden. Store in an airtight container.
Yield: 2 loaves bread

PANETTONE

1 package dry yeast
1/4 cup warm water
1 cup milk
1/2 cup butter or margarine
1/3 cup sugar
2 eggs
2 egg yolks
1 1/2 teaspoons vanilla extract
1 teaspoon grated lemon zest
1/2 teaspoon salt
4 1/2 to 5 cups all-purpose flour,
divided
1 cup dried currants
1/2 cup diced candied orange peel
Vegetable cooking spray
1 1/2 tablespoons butter or margarine,
melted

In a small bowl, dissolve yeast in warm water. Combine milk, butter, and sugar in a small saucepan over medium heat. Stirring frequently, cook about 5 minutes or until butter melts and sugar dissolves. Remove from heat. In a large bowl, beat eggs, egg yolks, vanilla, lemon zest, and salt until well blended. Add yeast mixture and milk mixture to egg mixture. Add 4 cups flour, currants, and orange peel; stir until a soft dough forms. Turn dough onto a lightly floured surface. Knead 6 minutes or until dough becomes smooth and elastic, using additional flour as necessary. Place in a large bowl sprayed with cooking spray, turning once to coat top of dough. Cover and let rise in a warm place (80 to 85 degrees) 2 hours or until doubled in size.

Make collars of greased parchment paper to extend 3 inches above tops of two 7-inch-diameter by 2 3/4-inch-deep baking pans (use springform pans or soufflé dishes). Turn dough onto a lightly floured surface and punch down. Divide dough in half and place in prepared pans. Lightly cover with greased plastic wrap and let rise in a warm place about 1 1/2 hours or until doubled in size.

Preheat oven to 350 degrees. Bake on lower rack of oven 10 minutes. Reduce temperature to 325 degrees and bake 25 to 35 minutes or until bread is golden brown and a wooden skewer inserted in center of dough comes out clean. Cover with aluminum foil if bread browns too quickly. Cool in pans 10 minutes. Remove from pans and transfer to a wire rack. Brush with melted butter. Serve warm or cool completely. Store in an airtight container.
Yield: 2 loaves bread

A luscious cherry glaze is spooned over Maraschino Cherry Bread (bottom) for scrumptious snacking. Packed with currants and candied orange peel, Panettone is an Italian favorite served at Christmastime.

ZUCCHINI CORN BREAD

- 3 cups cornmeal
- 1/2 cup all-purpose flour
- 2 teaspoons baking powder
- 1 teaspoon salt
- 1 1/2 cups cottage cheese
- 1 1/2 cups milk
- 1 cup butter or margarine, melted
- 4 eggs
- 1 cup finely chopped zucchini
- 1 cup finely chopped onion

Preheat oven to 375 degrees. In a large bowl, combine cornmeal, flour, baking powder, and salt. In a medium bowl, whisk cottage cheese, milk, butter, and eggs. Add cottage cheese mixture, zucchini, and onion to dry ingredients; stir just until moistened. Pour into 2 greased 8-inch square baking pans. Bake 25 to 30 minutes or until golden brown. Cool completely in pans. Cover and refrigerate until ready to give. Give with serving instructions.
Yield: 2 pans corn bread
To serve: Preheat oven to 350 degrees. Cover and bake 30 to 35 minutes or until heated through. Serve warm.

Featuring a mild flavor that complements almost any meal, Zucchini Corn Bread is ideal for holiday gift-giving. Zucchini and onion add garden-fresh goodness to the moist bread.

Terrific for sharing with a companion, a cup of tea made with spicy Orange-Nutmeg Tea Mix will lend holiday flavor to breakfast or teatime.

ORANGE-NUTMEG TEA MIX

- 1 cup unsweetened powdered instant tea
- 1 cup sugar
- 1 package (0.15 ounce) unsweetened orange-flavored soft drink mix
- 1 teaspoon ground nutmeg

In a small bowl, combine instant tea, sugar, soft drink mix, and nutmeg; stir until well blended. Store in an airtight container. Give with serving instructions.
Yield: about 1 2/3 cups tea mix
To serve: Pour 6 ounces hot or cold water over 2 tablespoons tea mix; stir until well blended.

KEEPING CAKE

For best flavor, make cake at least 1 week before giving.

- 3 cups fresh cranberries, divided
- ³/₄ cup granulated sugar
- ¹/₂ teaspoon grated orange zest
- 2¹/₄ cups all-purpose flour
- 2 cups firmly packed brown sugar
- 2 teaspoons ground cinnamon
- ¹/₂ teaspoon ground nutmeg
- ¹/₂ teaspoon ground allspice
- ¹/₄ teaspoon ground cloves
- 2 teaspoons baking soda
- 1 teaspoon salt
- 2 eggs
- ³/₄ cup sour cream
- ¹/₂ cup butter or margarine, melted
- 1 cup coarsely chopped pecans

Preheat oven to 350 degrees. In a large saucepan, combine 1¹/₂ cups cranberries, sugar, and orange zest. Bring to a boil and cook, stirring constantly, until berries pop and mixture thickens (about 5 minutes). Remove from heat. Chop remaining cranberries and add to cranberry mixture; cool.

In a large bowl, combine flour, brown sugar, cinnamon, nutmeg, allspice, cloves, baking soda, and salt. In another bowl, beat eggs with sour cream. Stir egg mixture into dry ingredients. Stir in butter, cranberry mixture, and pecans. Pour batter into 2 greased and floured 4¹/₂ x 8¹/₂-inch loaf pans. Bake 1 hour or until a toothpick inserted in center of cake comes out clean. Cool in pans 10 minutes. Remove from pans and cool completely on wire racks. Wrap cakes in aluminum foil and allow flavor to develop at least 1 week. The flavor will continue to improve over several weeks. The cakes will keep up to 3 months in a cool, dry place.
Yield: 2 cakes

Tangy cranberries, zesty orange peel, and a medley of spices blend together beautifully in this traditional Keeping Cake, which lasts nicely for up to three months. Garnished with artificial greenery, this good-tasting token of friendship is the perfect way to celebrate the joyous, sharing nature of Christmas.

153

DOGGIE BISCUITS

- 1 teaspoon instant beef bouillon
- 1/2 cup hot water
- 2 1/4 cups whole-wheat flour
- 1/2 cup nonfat dry milk powder
- 1/3 cup vegetable oil
- 1 jar (about 3 1/4 ounces) bacon-flavored pieces
- 1 tablespoon firmly packed brown sugar
- 1 egg

Preheat oven to 300 degrees. In a medium bowl, dissolve bouillon in water. Add flour, dry milk, oil, bacon-flavored pieces, brown sugar, and egg, stirring until well blended. On a lightly floured surface, use a floured rolling pin to roll out dough to 1/8-inch thickness. Use a 2-inch heart-shaped cookie cutter to cut out dough. Transfer to a greased baking sheet. Bake 30 to 35 minutes or until firm. Transfer to a wire rack to cool completely. Store in an airtight container.

Yield: about 6 dozen doggie biscuits

Even an old dog might learn a new trick for these wholesome heart-shaped Doggie Biscuits. The easy-to-fix canine treats are flavored with beef and bacon.

TWO-BERRY JAM

- 1/2 cup grape juice
- 1 cup frozen blackberries, thawed
- 1 cup frozen raspberries, thawed
- 4 cups sugar
- 1 pouch (3 ounces) liquid fruit pectin

In a large Dutch oven, combine grape juice, blackberries, raspberries, and sugar; stir until well blended. Let stand 10 minutes. Stirring constantly over high heat, bring mixture to a rolling boil. Stir in liquid pectin. Stirring constantly, bring to a rolling boil again and boil 1 minute longer. Remove from heat; skim foam from top. Spoon jam into heat-resistant jars; cover and cool to room temperature. Store in refrigerator.

Yield: about 2 pints jam

Two-Berry Jam, with its twin combination of blackberries and raspberries, has a sweet, fruity taste that's ideal with biscuits or English muffins.

APRICOT BREAD

¾ cup butter or margarine, softened
¾ cup sugar
2 eggs, lightly beaten
1 cup chopped dried apricots
½ cup toasted coconut
¼ cup orange juice
1 teaspoon grated orange zest
1 teaspoon ground cinnamon
3 cups all-purpose flour
1 teaspoon salt
1 teaspoon baking soda
1 cup sour cream
½ cup chopped walnuts

Preheat oven to 350 degrees. In a large bowl, cream butter and sugar until fluffy. Beat in eggs. Stir in apricots, coconut, orange juice, orange zest, and cinnamon. In a medium bowl, combine flour, salt, and baking soda. Alternately stir dry ingredients and sour cream into apricot mixture. Stir in walnuts. Pour batter into a greased 5 x 9 x 3-inch loaf pan. Bake 1 hour or until a toothpick inserted in center of bread comes out clean. Remove from pan and cool on wire rack. Store in an airtight container.
Yield: 1 loaf bread

LOW-CALORIE RASPBERRY SPREAD

1 teaspoon unflavored gelatin
¼ cup unsweetened apple juice
1 cup frozen raspberries, thawed and puréed
2½ teaspoons aspartame sweetener (8 packets)
¼ teaspoon ground cinnamon

Soften gelatin in apple juice in small saucepan. Place over medium-low heat and stir until gelatin dissolves and mixture simmers. Remove from heat and stir in puréed berries. Stir in sweetener and cinnamon. Pour into a half-pint jar with lid. Store in refrigerator.
Yield: about 1 cup spread

Here's a yummy trio of Christmas gifts that says "good cheer." Low-Calorie Raspberry Spread is a heavenly treat for the dieter. Served either hot or cold, Fruit Sip is a non-alcoholic drink that kids can enjoy, too. Apricot Bread, enriched with toasted coconut, is a wonderful snack.

FRUIT SIP

1 bottle (48 ounces) apple-cherry juice
3 three-inch-long cinnamon sticks
½ cup chopped dried apples
½ cup chopped dates
½ cup raisins
2 teaspoons vanilla extract

In a large saucepan, combine juice, cinnamon sticks, apples, dates, raisins, and vanilla. Bring to a simmer and remove from heat. Allow to cool. Cover and chill overnight.

Drain the liquid through a strainer or doubled layer of cheesecloth into a bowl. Pour liquid into a glass bottle with lid. Serve hot or cold. Store in refrigerator.
Yield: six 8-ounce servings

Crowned with glazed walnuts and apricots, Fruited Cheesecake gives Christmas fruitcake a fresh, new image. The creamy filling, nestled in a gingersnap crust, features apricots, walnuts, dates, and prunes.

FRUITED CHEESECAKE

CHEESECAKE
1 cup chopped dried apricots, plus 10 whole dried apricots
1/2 cup brandy
1 1/3 cups gingersnap cookie crumbs
1/4 cup butter or margarine, melted
2/3 cup chopped prunes
2/3 cup chopped dates
1 cup coarsely chopped walnuts
2 tablespoons all-purpose flour

3 packages (8 ounces each) cream cheese, softened
1 cup sugar
4 eggs

TOPPING
1 1/2 cups sour cream
1/2 cup apricot preserves, divided
1 tablespoon brandy
1/3 cup coarsely chopped walnuts
1 tablespoon butter or margarine

For cheesecake, place apricots in a shallow bowl. Add brandy, cover, and let sit at room temperature overnight.

Preheat oven to 375 degrees. Line bottom of a 9-inch springform pan with aluminum foil, wrapping edges under bottom of pan. Combine cookie crumbs and butter. Press into bottom and 1 inch up sides of pan.

Drain apricots, reserving brandy. Set aside whole apricots for garnish. In a

156

medium bowl, combine chopped apricots, prunes, dates, and 1 cup walnuts; toss with flour. In a separate bowl, beat cream cheese until fluffy. Add sugar gradually, mixing well. Add eggs, 1 at a time, beating after each addition. Fold in fruit mixture and reserved brandy. Pour into pan and bake 45 to 50 minutes or until set.

For topping, combine sour cream, 2 tablespoons preserves, and brandy in a small bowl. Spread over cheesecake and bake 5 minutes longer. Allow cake to cool to room temperature. Refrigerate at least 12 hours.

In a small saucepan, melt remaining preserves. Reserving a small amount for garnish, spread preserves over top of cheesecake.

To garnish, sauté walnuts in butter 5 minutes. Drain on a paper towel. Slice reserved whole apricots lengthwise. Remove sides of springform pan. Use foil lining to gently lift cake from bottom of pan onto a 10-inch-diameter piece of cardboard. Referring to photo, arrange apricots and walnuts on top of cake. Glaze with remaining melted preserves. Store in an airtight container in refrigerator.
Yield: 10 to 12 servings

PECAN BUTTER SPREAD

1¼ cups chopped pecans
2 tablespoons peanut oil
8 ounces Brie cheese, rind
      removed
1 package (3 ounces) cream
      cheese, softened
2 tablespoons sherry
¼ teaspoon salt
   Crackers or apples and Roasted
      Pecans to serve

Process pecans and peanut oil in a food processor until smooth. Add Brie cheese, cream cheese, sherry, and salt; process until mixture is completely blended. Store in an airtight container in refrigerator. Serve at room temperature with crackers or apple slices topped with Roasted Pecans.
Yield: about 1½ cups spread

Spread goodwill to someone dear with a jar of Pecan Butter Spread. It's luscious on crackers, especially when topped with Roasted Pecans.

ROASTED PECANS

1 cup pecan halves
1 tablespoon butter, melted
   Salt

Preheat oven to 200 degrees. In a small bowl, combine pecans and butter. Pour nuts onto a baking sheet and bake 1 hour, stirring every 15 minutes. Drain on paper towel; sprinkle with salt. Cool completely. Store in an airtight container.
Yield: 1 cup pecans

157

This Christmas, send a sweet assortment of special delivery gifts to your favorite friends! Our Butterscotch Bars (from left) are crowned with pecans and ice-cream topping. Cream Syrup (in large jar) is an elegant complement to warm breakfast foods like French toast. Embellished with red string candy bows, Candy Wreath Ornaments are a crispy treat made with crushed shredded wheat biscuits. Delicious on toast or English muffins, Banana Butter (at right) is seasoned with pumpkin pie spice.

CANDY WREATH ORNAMENTS

3¹/₂ cups miniature marshmallows
¹/₄ cup butter or margarine
9 large shredded wheat biscuits, crushed
3 ounces vanilla candy coating
Red string licorice and small red cinnamon candies to decorate

In a large saucepan, melt marshmallows and butter, stirring until smooth. Stir in crushed biscuits. To make each wreath, shape ¹/₄ cup mixture into a small ball. Flatten ball with palm of hand. Cut out center with a 1¹/₂-inch biscuit cutter. Melt candy coating in a heavy small saucepan over low heat. Remove from heat. Transfer to a heavy-duty resealable plastic bag. Cut a small hole in 1 corner of bag. Referring to photo, drizzle melted candy coating onto wreaths. Tie licorice in bows. Attach bows and cinnamon candies with melted candy coating.
Yield: about 1¹/₂ dozen wreaths

BUTTERSCOTCH BARS

1 cup all-purpose flour
1 cup quick-cooking rolled oats
³/₄ cup firmly packed brown sugar
²/₃ cup butter or margarine, melted
¹/₂ teaspoon baking soda
¹/₄ teaspoon salt
1 cup butterscotch chips
²/₃ cup chopped pecans, divided
²/₃ cup butterscotch ice-cream topping
2 tablespoons all-purpose flour

Preheat oven to 350 degrees. In a large bowl, combine 1 cup flour, oats, brown sugar, butter, baking soda, and salt. Press two-thirds of oat mixture into a greased 8-inch square baking pan. Bake 10 minutes. Remove from oven and sprinkle with butterscotch chips and ¹/₃ cup pecans. In a small bowl, mix ice-cream topping and 2 tablespoons flour; drizzle over butterscotch chips and pecans. Sprinkle with remaining oat mixture and pecans. Bake 15 to 20 minutes or until lightly browned. Cool completely. Cut into bars.
Yield: about 2 dozen bars

CREAM SYRUP

2 cups sugar
2 cups light corn syrup
2 cups whipping cream
1 teaspoon freshly grated nutmeg

In a Dutch oven, combine sugar, corn syrup, and whipping cream. Bring mixture to a boil; boil 3 minutes, stirring constantly. Remove from heat and stir in nutmeg. Serve warm with French toast, pancakes, or waffles. Store in an airtight container in refrigerator.
Yield: about 4 cups syrup

BANANA BUTTER

4 large ripe bananas, peeled and sliced
3 tablespoons lemon juice
1 1/2 cups sugar
1 teaspoon pumpkin pie spice

Process bananas and lemon juice in a food processor until smooth. Transfer bananas to a large saucepan and stir in sugar and pumpkin pie spice. Bring mixture to a boil. Stirring frequently, lower heat and simmer 15 minutes. Spoon into heat-resistant jars; cover and cool to room temperature. Serve on toast or English muffins. Store in refrigerator.
Yield: about 3 cups banana butter

HONEY-CHEESE ROLLS

8 cups all-purpose flour, divided
2 teaspoons salt
2 packages dry yeast
3/4 cup butter or margarine, divided
2 cups (8 ounces) shredded Cheddar cheese
1 1/2 cups milk
1/3 cup honey
3 eggs

In a large bowl, combine 6 cups flour, salt, and yeast; stir until well blended. In a medium saucepan, combine 1/2 cup butter, cheese, milk, and honey. Cook over medium heat until a thermometer registers

The wonderfully mild flavor of Honey-Cheese Rolls will delight any bread lovers on your gift list. Shredded Cheddar and golden honey enliven the yeast rolls.

130 degrees (butter may not be completely melted). Add eggs and cheese mixture alternately to dry ingredients, stirring until a soft dough forms. Gradually stir in remaining flour. Turn dough onto a lightly floured surface; knead about 10 minutes or until dough becomes soft and elastic. Transfer to a large greased bowl. Melt remaining 1/4 cup butter in a small saucepan over low heat. Brush top of dough with half of melted butter and cover. Let rise in a warm place (80 to 85 degrees) 1 hour or until doubled in size.

Turn dough onto a lightly floured surface and punch down. Shape dough into 3-inch balls and place with sides touching in greased 9-inch round cake pans. If necessary, remelt remaining butter. Brush tops of rolls with melted butter and cover. Let rise about 1 hour or until doubled in size.

Preheat oven to 375 degrees. Bake 30 to 35 minutes or until golden brown. Cool completely in pan. Store in an airtight container. Give with serving instructions.
Yield: about 2 dozen rolls
To serve: Preheat oven to 350 degrees. Bake rolls, uncovered, 3 to 5 minutes or until heated through.

With our easy-to-follow decorating tips, it's a snap to transform store-bought cookies into fun treats. Purchased icing, cinnamon candies, and shiny dragées turn plain cookies into holly-trimmed Wreath Cookies and poinsettia-adorned Gift Box Cookies. Cookies dipped in candy coating and topped with almond "flames" stand upright on chocolate sandwich cookies to make our unique Candle Cookies.

CANDLE COOKIES

    Vanilla candy coating
1   package (5¹/₂ ounces) Pepperidge Farms Pirouette cookies
    Purchased green decorating icing
    Chocolate sandwich cookies
    Whole almonds

Melt candy coating in a small saucepan according to package directions. Using tongs, dip each Pirouette cookie into candy coating. Place on a wire rack with waxed paper underneath; let coating harden.

Using a large star tip, pipe icing in a small circle onto 1 side of each sandwich cookie. Press 1 end of a dipped cookie into icing. Using a small amount of icing, secure 1 almond in remaining end of dipped cookie. Allow icing to harden. Store in an airtight container.
Yield: about 1¹/₂ dozen cookies

WREATH COOKIES

1   package (11 ounces) wreath-shaped cookies
    Purchased green decorating icing
    Small red cinnamon candies

Using a small leaf tip, pipe icing onto each cookie to resemble leaves. Place candies in center of leaves. Allow icing to harden. Store in an airtight container.
Yield: about 2¹/₂ dozen cookies

GIFT BOX COOKIES

1   package (10 ounces) square shortbread cookies
    Purchased red and green decorating icing
    Gold dragées (for decoration only)

Using a small leaf tip, pipe green icing onto each cookie to resemble ribbon. Using a small round tip, pipe red icing onto each cookie to resemble a poinsettia. Place a dragée in center of each flower. Allow icing to harden. Store in an airtight container. Remove dragées before eating cookies.
Yield: about 3¹/₂ dozen cookies

CHEESE STRAWS

 2 cups all-purpose flour
 1/2 cup butter or margarine, melted
 1 1/2 teaspoons salt
 3/4 teaspoon ground red pepper
 4 cups (16 ounces) finely
 shredded sharp Cheddar
 cheese

Preheat oven to 350 degrees. In a medium bowl, combine flour, melted butter, salt, and red pepper. Add cheese; mix with a pastry blender until well blended. Place dough in a cookie press fitted with a 1 1/2-inch ribbon disk. Press dough in long strips onto an ungreased baking sheet. Cut strips into 3 1/2-inch lengths. Bake 8 to 9 minutes or until bottoms are lightly browned. Transfer cheese straws to a wire rack to cool. Store in a cookie tin.
Yield: about 7 1/2 dozen cheese straws

PICKLED ONIONS

 8 pints pearl onions (about
 5 pounds), peeled
 3/4 cup salt
 7 cups white vinegar (5% acidity)
 1 cup sugar
 Small bay leaves
 Whole red peppercorns
 Whole green peppercorns
 Mustard seed

Place onions in a large bowl; sprinkle with salt. Cover onions with water. Cover and refrigerate overnight.
 Combine vinegar and sugar in a small stockpot over high heat; bring to a boil. Reduce heat and keep mixture hot. Drain onions and rinse with cold water. Fill heat-resistant jars with onions. Add a bay leaf and 1 teaspoon each of red peppercorns, green peppercorns, and mustard seed to each jar. Add hot vinegar mixture to each jar. Cover and cool to room temperature. Store in refrigerator.
Yield: about 12 half-pints onions

Light, tasty Cheese Straws are quick to fix with a cookie press. A touch of red pepper adds a wonderfully piquant flavor to the snacks.

Packed with zesty old-fashioned goodness, Pickled Onions are seasoned with colorful peppercorns and mustard seed.

For a perfect hostess gift, take along a tin of irresistible Sticky Buns. These sweet yeast rolls are filled with cinnamon and raisins and topped with a honey glaze of brown sugar and pecans.

STICKY BUNS

2 packages dry yeast
1/3 cup granulated sugar
1 teaspoon salt
1/4 cup milk
1/2 cup buttermilk
1 tablespoon orange juice
1/2 teaspoon grated orange zest
1 teaspoon vanilla extract
2 egg yolks
3 cups all-purpose flour, divided
1 cup butter or margarine, softened
4 teaspoons ground cinnamon
1 cup raisins
2 cups firmly packed brown
    sugar, divided
1/2 cup honey
1 cup chopped pecans
1/4 cup butter or margarine, melted

In a large bowl, combine yeast, granulated sugar, and salt. Beat in milk, buttermilk, orange juice, orange zest, and vanilla until smooth. Stir in egg yolks and 1 1/2 cups of flour. Stir in butter and remaining 1 1/2 cups flour. On a lightly floured surface, knead dough until smooth and elastic (about 10 minutes). Place dough in a lightly greased bowl. Cover and chill 2 hours or until well chilled.

Preheat oven to 350 degrees. On a lightly floured surface, knead dough again until smooth. Using a floured rolling pin, roll out dough into a 1/4-inch-thick rectangle about 10 x 18 inches. Sprinkle with cinnamon, raisins, and 1 cup brown sugar. Beginning at 1 long edge, roll up dough jellyroll style. Cut into 3/4-inch-thick slices.

In a small bowl, combine the remaining 1 cup brown sugar, honey, and pecans. Grease four 6-cup jumbo muffin tins. Place 1 tablespoon pecan mixture in each muffin cup. Place a slice of dough on top of pecan mixture. Brush tops of dough with melted butter. Bake 35 to 40 minutes or until golden brown. Turn sticky buns onto waxed paper to cool completely. Store in an airtight container.
Yield: 2 dozen buns

RASPBERRY FUDGE BROWNIES

- ½ cup butter or margarine, softened
- 1 cup sugar
- 3 eggs
- 1 jar (12 ounces) raspberry jam, divided
- 18 chocolate wafer cookies (2-inch diameter), finely ground
- ½ cup all-purpose flour
- 1 cup (6 ounces) semisweet chocolate chips
- 1 cup chopped walnuts

Preheat oven to 350 degrees. In a large bowl, cream butter and sugar until fluffy. Add eggs and ½ cup jam, beating until smooth. Add ground cookies and flour; mix well. Pour batter into a greased 8 x 11-inch baking dish. Sprinkle chocolate chips evenly over batter. Bake 35 to 40 minutes or until a toothpick inserted in center comes out clean. In a small saucepan, melt remaining jam over low heat, stirring constantly. Stir in walnuts. Pour jam mixture over brownies. Cool completely in pan. Cut into 2-inch squares. Store in an airtight container.
Yield: about 1½ dozen brownies

Lift holiday spirits with a gift of homemade Coffee Liqueur, which is especially appealing when served from purchased chocolate liqueur cups. The flavorful concoction can also be stirred into coffee or poured over ice cream for a special dessert.

Raspberry Fudge Brownies make mouth-watering Christmas treats! Walnuts and raspberry jam enhance the rich, moist brownies.

COFFEE LIQUEUR

- 6 cups sugar
- ½ cup instant coffee granules
- 2½ quarts boiling water
- 1 bottle (750 ml) pure grain alcohol
- ¼ cup vanilla extract

In a large bowl, combine sugar and coffee. Add boiling water, stirring to dissolve. Cool completely. Stir in pure grain alcohol and vanilla. Pour mixture into bottles and close tightly. Let stand in a dark place for at least 2 weeks before serving.
Yield: about 16 cups liqueur

Entice the chocolate lovers on your list with sumptuous Brandied Fruit Balls. The elegant candies are created by coating a nutty blend of brandy and dried fruit with melted chocolate.

BRANDIED FRUIT BALLS

1 pound dried fruit (we used a mixture of cherries, peaches, dates, prunes, cranberries, and apricots)
1 cup chopped walnuts
¼ cup brandy
½ cup sifted confectioners sugar
¾ cup semisweet chocolate chips
7 ounces chocolate candy coating, chopped

Process dried fruit, walnuts, and brandy in a food processor until finely chopped. Chill in an airtight container 1 hour.

Shape brandied fruit into 1-inch balls; roll lightly in confectioners sugar and place on a baking sheet. In a heavy medium saucepan over low heat, melt chocolate chips and candy coating. Remove chocolate from heat.

Placing each fruit ball on a fork and holding over saucepan, spoon chocolate over balls. Transfer to a baking sheet covered with waxed paper. Chill until chocolate hardens. Store in an airtight container in refrigerator.

Yield: about 4 dozen fruit balls

BRANDIED STRAWBERRIES

1½ cups firmly packed brown
     sugar
1 cup water
1 package (16 ounces) frozen
    unsweetened strawberries,
    thawed and drained
¼ cup lemon juice
½ cup brandy
    Pound cake to serve

In a large saucepan, combine brown sugar and water. Stirring constantly, cook over medium heat until sugar dissolves. Stir in strawberries and lemon juice. Bring to a boil and cook 10 minutes. Remove from heat; stir in brandy. Store in an airtight container in refrigerator. Serve with cake or ice cream.

Yield: about 1½ pints strawberries

Brandied Strawberries can't be beat as a spirited finale to a holiday meal. Spooned over cake or ice cream, the colorful mixture is an Epicurean delight!

CINNAMON DIP

1 package (8 ounces) cream
    cheese, softened
2 tablespoons milk
1 teaspoon vanilla extract
2 tablespoons firmly packed
    brown sugar
1 teaspoon ground cinnamon
¼ teaspoon ground nutmeg
    Apples or cookies to serve

In a medium bowl, beat cream cheese, milk, vanilla extract, brown sugar, cinnamon, and nutmeg until smooth. Store in an airtight container in refrigerator. Serve with apple slices or cookies.

Yield: about 1 cup dip

Paired with a shiny red apple, creamy Cinnamon Dip is an appetizing way to show appreciation to a favorite teacher. Great on slices of fresh fruit, this delicately flavored dip is sure to rate an A⁺!

STOLLEN

BREAD

- 1 package dry yeast
- 1/4 cup warm water
- 3 to 3 1/2 cups all-purpose flour, divided
- 1/2 teaspoon salt
- 1/2 teaspoon ground nutmeg
- 1/8 teaspoon ground cardamom
- 2/3 cup butter or margarine
- 1/2 cup plus 2 teaspoons milk, divided
- 1/4 cup sugar
- 2 eggs
- 1 teaspoon grated lemon zest
- 1 cup chopped red candied cherries
- 2/3 cup slivered almonds, toasted
- 1/4 cup golden raisins
- 1/4 cup chopped candied citrus peel
  Vegetable cooking spray
- 1 egg

ICING

- 1 cup sifted confectioners sugar
- 2 1/2 teaspoons water
- 1 teaspoon brandy

For bread, dissolve yeast in warm water in a small bowl. In a medium bowl, combine 3 cups flour, salt, nutmeg, and cardamom. In a small saucepan, heat butter, 1/2 cup milk, and sugar over medium-low heat until butter melts and sugar dissolves. Remove from heat and cool to lukewarm.

In a large bowl, lightly beat 2 eggs. Stir in yeast mixture, milk mixture, and lemon zest. Stir in flour mixture until a soft dough forms. Turn onto a lightly floured surface and knead 5 minutes or until dough becomes smooth and elastic. Gradually add cherries, almonds, raisins, and citrus peel; knead until ingredients are well distributed, using additional flour as necessary. Place in a large bowl sprayed with cooking spray, turning once to coat top of dough. Cover and let rise in a warm place (80 to 85 degrees) 2 hours or until doubled in size.

Turn dough onto a lightly floured surface and punch down. On a lightly greased baking sheet, shape dough into an 8 x 12-inch flattened oval. Fold dough in half lengthwise. Spray top of dough with cooking spray, cover, and let rise in a warm place about 1 1/2 hours or until doubled in size.

Preheat oven to 350 degrees. Beat 1 egg and remaining 2 teaspoons milk in a small bowl until well blended; brush over entire loaf. Bake 30 to 40 minutes or until loaf is golden brown and sounds hollow when tapped. Cover with aluminum foil if top browns too quickly. Transfer loaf to a wire rack with waxed paper underneath to cool completely.

For icing, combine confectioners sugar and water in a medium bowl. Add brandy; stir until smooth. Pour icing over loaf. Allow icing to harden. Store in an airtight container.

Yield: 1 loaf bread

Friends will appreciate receiving savory Cheddar Spread, a smooth blend of cheeses enhanced with sherry and zesty spices.

CHEDDAR SPREAD

- 1 package (8 ounces) cream cheese, softened
- 2 cups (8 ounces) shredded sharp Cheddar cheese
- 1/3 cup sherry
- 1/2 teaspoon garlic powder
- 1/2 teaspoon salt
- 1/4 teaspoon ground white pepper
- 1/4 teaspoon dry mustard
  Crackers or bread to serve

In a large bowl, beat cream cheese until fluffy. Add Cheddar cheese, sherry, garlic powder, salt, white pepper, and dry mustard; beat until well blended. Transfer to an airtight container and refrigerate 8 hours or overnight to allow flavors to blend. Store in refrigerator. Give with serving instructions.

Yield: about 2 cups spread

To serve: Let stand at room temperature 20 to 30 minutes or until softened. Serve with crackers or bread.

A popular German yeast bread, Stollen is a nutty, fruity combination laced with nutmeg and cardamom. Our loaf is drenched with a sweet, spirited icing.

MICROWAVE ROCKY ROAD FUDGE

4½ cups sifted confectioners sugar
½ cup butter or margarine
⅓ cup cocoa
¼ cup milk
¼ teaspoon salt
½ cup chopped pecans
½ cup miniature marshmallows
1 teaspoon vanilla extract

Line an 8-inch square baking pan with aluminum foil, extending foil over 2 sides of pan; grease foil. In a large microwave-safe bowl, combine confectioners sugar, butter, cocoa, milk, and salt. Microwave on high power (100%) 2 to 2½ minutes or until butter is melted. Add pecans, marshmallows, and vanilla; stir until well blended. Pour into prepared pan. Chill about 1 hour or until firm. Use ends of foil to lift candy from pan. Cut into 1-inch squares and store in an airtight container.
Yield: about 1½ pounds fudge

A classic confection, Microwave Rocky Road Fudge requires only a handful of ingredients and whips up quickly in the microwave. In no time, you'll have a chocolaty, marshmallowy delight that's too good to keep to yourself!

For a refreshingly different Yuletide gift, surprise a special someone with a jar of Peppermint Stick Sauce. The creamy sauce lends minty taste and pretty pink color to a scoop of ice cream.

PEPPERMINT STICK SAUCE

1½ cups finely crushed peppermint candies
1½ cups whipping cream
1 jar (7 ounces) marshmallow creme

In a medium saucepan, combine candies, whipping cream, and marshmallow creme. Stirring constantly with a wooden spoon, cook over medium heat until smooth. Remove from heat. Pour into an airtight container and refrigerate. Serve chilled over ice cream or cake.
Yield: about 2 cups sauce

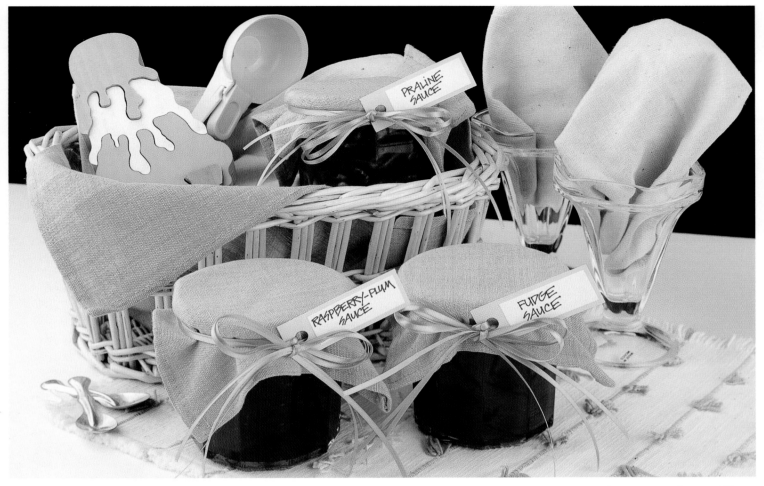

Help a friend create taste-tempting treats with our three scrumptious ice-cream toppings. Raspberry-Plum Sauce, Fudge Sauce, and Praline Sauce feature flavors that appeal to serious sundae lovers. One jar of the sauce makes a nice gift, or give a sampling of all three.

RASPBERRY-PLUM SAUCE

  2 tablespoons cold water
  4 teaspoons cornstarch
  2 packages (12 ounces each)
      frozen raspberries, thawed
1^1/$_3$ cups red plum jelly

In a small bowl, combine water and cornstarch; set aside. Combine raspberries and jelly in a large saucepan over medium-high heat. Bring to a boil, stirring constantly. Blend cornstarch mixture into raspberry mixture. Stirring constantly, cook 3 minutes or until sauce thickens; cool. To remove seeds, place sauce in a fine-mesh strainer and push sauce through strainer with back of a spoon. Discard seeds. Store sauce in an airtight container in refrigerator. Serve warm.
Yield: about 4 cups sauce

FUDGE SAUCE

  1 package (12 ounces)
      semisweet chocolate chips
  1 cup butter or margarine
  4 cups (1 pound) confectioners
      sugar
2^2/$_3$ cups evaporated milk
2^1/$_2$ teaspoons vanilla extract
  ^{1}/$_8$ teaspoon salt

Combine chocolate chips and butter in a large saucepan over low heat. Stir constantly until melted. Gradually add sugar and evaporated milk, blending well. Increase heat. Stirring constantly, bring to a boil and cook 8 minutes. Remove from heat. Stir in vanilla and salt. Store in an airtight container in refrigerator. Serve warm.
Yield: about 5^1/$_2$ cups sauce

PRALINE SAUCE

2^1/$_2$ cups firmly packed dark
      brown sugar
1^1/$_3$ cups light corn syrup
  ^{1}/$_2$ cup butter or margarine
  ^{1}/$_2$ cup evaporated milk
1^1/$_2$ teaspoons vanilla extract
  2 cups pecan halves

Combine brown sugar, corn syrup, and butter in top of a double boiler over boiling water. Stirring constantly, cook about 8 to 10 minutes or until sauce thickens. Remove from heat and cool slightly. Stir in evaporated milk, vanilla, and pecan halves. Store in an airtight container in refrigerator. Serve warm.
Yield: about 4 cups sauce

An adorable basket of Gingerbread and Custard Sauce is the sweetest way we know to brighten someone's day. For a charming touch, dress up your homemade gingerbread boy with miniature marshmallows and a plaid bow.

GINGERBREAD

- 1 cup vegetable shortening
- 1/2 cup sugar
- 2 eggs
- 1 cup light molasses
- 1 cup maple syrup
- 2 cups boiling water
- 4 1/2 cups all-purpose flour
- 2 teaspoons baking soda
- 1 teaspoon salt
- 2 teaspoons ground ginger
- 2 teaspoons ground cinnamon
- 1/2 teaspoon ground mace
  Custard Sauce to serve

Preheat oven to 325 degrees. Grease and flour a 9 x 13 x 2-inch baking pan or an 11-inch-long gingerbread boy-shaped baking pan. In a large bowl, cream shortening, sugar, and eggs. Beat in molasses, syrup, and water. Sift together dry ingredients; stir into molasses mixture. Pour into pan and bake 35 to 45 minutes or until cake springs back when lightly touched in center. Cool in pan 10 minutes. Remove from pan and cool completely on a wire rack. Serve with warm Custard Sauce. Store cake in an airtight container.

Yield: 10 to 12 servings

CUSTARD SAUCE

- 6 egg yolks, lightly beaten
- 2 cups whipping cream
- 3 tablespoons firmly packed brown sugar
- 2 tablespoons butter or margarine
- 2 teaspoons vanilla extract

Place egg yolks, whipping cream, and brown sugar in top of a double boiler over hot (not boiling) water. Cook, stirring constantly, until thick and creamy. Add butter. Remove from heat and stir in vanilla. Store in an airtight container in refrigerator. To serve, heat in double boiler over simmering water.

Yield: about 2 cups sauce

APPLE-CINNAMON-NUT BREAD

1½ cups all-purpose flour
1 cup sugar, divided
½ cup chopped pecans
1½ teaspoons baking powder
½ teaspoon salt
½ teaspoon ground cinnamon
⅓ cup vegetable oil
1 egg
¼ cup orange juice
1 teaspoon vanilla extract
1 medium Granny Smith apple, peeled, cored, and thinly sliced

Preheat oven to 350 degrees. In a medium bowl, combine flour, ¾ cup sugar, pecans, baking powder, and salt. Combine remaining ¼ cup sugar and cinnamon in a small bowl; set aside. In another small bowl, whisk oil, egg, orange juice, and vanilla. Add oil mixture to dry ingredients; stir just until moistened. Spread half of batter into 4 greased and floured 2½ x 5-inch loaf pans. Place a single layer of apple slices over batter. Sprinkle cinnamon-sugar mixture over apples. Spread remaining batter over apples. Bake 30 to 35 minutes or until a toothpick inserted in center of bread comes out clean and tops are lightly browned. Cool bread in pans on a wire rack 10 minutes. Transfer bread to wire rack to cool completely. Store in an airtight container.

Yield: 4 mini bread loaves

Moist, delicious Apple-Cinnamon-Nut Bread is a memorable gift that will earn high marks with teachers! Each little loaf is packed with crunchy pecans and features a mouth-watering layer of apples and cinnamon.

For a Yuletide offering with European flavor, present a bottle of Pear Wine. Wonderful served with fresh bread sticks or cheese, the mellow beverage is easy to make by adding fresh fruit and sugar to white wine.

172

PEAR WINE

- 4 ripe Bartlett pears
- 1 bottle (750 ml) dry white wine
- 1/4 cup sugar

Wash and core pears; cut into small cubes. Combine pears, wine, and sugar in a large glass bowl; stir until sugar dissolves. Pour into wine bottle and chill 3 days to allow flavors to blend. Serve chilled.
Yield: about 3 cups wine

CHERRY DIVINITY

- 2 cups sugar
- 1/2 cup light corn syrup
- 1/2 cup water
- 1/8 teaspoon salt
- 2 egg whites
- 1 teaspoon vanilla extract
- 1 cup chopped red candied cherries
- 1/2 cup finely chopped walnuts

Line an 8-inch square baking pan with aluminum foil, extending foil over 2 sides of pan. Butter sides of a heavy large saucepan. Combine sugar, corn syrup, water, and salt in pan over medium-low heat, stirring constantly until sugar dissolves (syrup will become clear). Using a pastry brush dipped in hot water, wash down any sugar crystals on sides of pan. Attach candy thermometer to pan, making sure thermometer does not touch bottom of pan. Increase heat to medium and bring to a boil. Do not stir while syrup is boiling.

When syrup reaches approximately 240 degrees, beat egg whites in a large bowl until stiff using highest speed of an electric mixer; set aside.

Continue to cook syrup until it reaches firm-ball stage (approximately 242 to 248 degrees). Test about 1/2 teaspoon syrup in ice water. Syrup will form a firm ball in ice water but flatten if pressed when removed from the water. While beating egg whites at low speed, slowly pour syrup into egg whites. Add vanilla and increase speed of mixer to high. Continue to beat until

Light, fluffy Cherry Divinity is a divine way to tell friends "You're extra special." The homemade treats are accented with chopped cherries.

candy is no longer glossy and a stationary column forms when beaters are lifted. Fold in cherries and walnuts. Pour into prepared pan. Allow to harden. Use ends of foil to lift candy from pan. Cut into 1-inch squares. Store in an airtight container.
Yield: about 5 dozen squares divinity

173

INDEX